# I
# Jennifer
# Coolidge

# I ❤ Jennifer Coolidge

## A Celebration of Your Favorite Pop Culture Icon

LAUREN EMILY WHALEN

Illustrated by Neryl Walker

RUNNING PRESS

PHILADELPHIA

Running Press
Hachette Book Group
1290 Avenue of the Americas, New York, NY 10104
www.runningpress.com
@Running_Press

First Edition: April 2024

Published by Running Press, an imprint of Hachette Book Group, Inc. The Running Press name and logo are trademarks of Hachette Book Group, Inc.

The Hachette Speakers Bureau provides a wide range of authors for speaking events. To find out more, go to www.hachettespeakersbureau.com or email HachetteSpeakers@hbgusa.com.

Running Press books may be purchased in bulk for business, educational, or promotional use. For more information, please contact your local bookseller or the Hachette Book Group Special Markets Department at Special.Markets@hbgusa.com.

The publisher is not responsible for websites (or their content) that are not owned by the publisher.

Print book cover and interior design by Susan Van Horn.

Library of Congress Cataloging-in-Publication Data
Names: Whalen, Lauren Emily, author. | Walker, Neryl, illustrator.
Title: I [heart] Jennifer Coolidge : a celebration of your favorite pop culture icon / Lauren Emily Whalen ; illustrated by Neryl Walker.
Description: First edition. | Philadelphia : Running Press, Hachette Book Group, 2024. | The word "heart" appears as a heart symbol on title page. | Includes bibliographical references.
Identifiers: LCCN 2023035337 (print) | LCCN 2023035338 (ebook) | ISBN 9780762486373 (hardcover) | ISBN 9780762486380 (ebook)
Subjects: LCSH: Coolidge, Jennifer—Miscellanea. | Actresses—United States—Miscellanea.
Classification: LCC PN2287.C5875 W47 2024  (print) | LCC PN2287.C5875 (ebook) |
DDC 792.02/8092 [B]—dc23/eng/20231129
LC record available at https://lccn.loc.gov/2023035337
LC ebook record available at https://lccn.loc.gov/2023035338

ISBNs: 978-0-7624-8637-3 (hardcover), 978-0-7624-8638-0 (ebook)

Printed in the United States of America

LSC-C

Printing 1, 2024

# Contents

# Introduction, or
# Why I ♥ Jennifer Coolidge

The first time I saw Jennifer Coolidge was in *American Pie,* in a small but incredibly pivotal breakout role as Stifler's Mom, the leggy blonde cougar in a skintight blue dress with a propensity for Scotch—essentially 1999's very own Mrs. Robinson.

But the first time I really *remember* Jennifer Coolidge happened the next year, when I saw a little movie called *Best in Show* at my neighborhood art house theater in Chicago. Among a plethora of memorable characters—quirky canine owners from across the country, each vying for their pooch to take the grand prize in the fictional Mayflower Kennel Club Dog Show—Jen stood out as Sherri Ann Cabot, a ditzy trophy wife whose relationship with her purebred poodle's handler, Christy Cummings, played by the indomitable Jane Lynch, might be a bit . . . more than friendly.

At first I didn't realize this actress was also Stifler's Mom, but I thought she was absolutely hilarious, from her introduction alongside her decrepit husband, when she seriously informs the camera, "We both love soup," to Sherri Ann's final scene, when she proudly unveils *American Bitch* magazine for lesbian dog owners alongside her new partner—none other than Christy Cummings.

Several months after *Best in Show,* I sat down at my hometown movie theater with my mom and sister to watch a new studio movie called *Legally Blonde.* The three of us adored Reese Witherspoon as the peppy, scrappy Elle Woods and cracked up when Paulette Bonafonté was introduced—Elle's manicurist and confidante who's devoted to her dog, Rufus, and can't help but crush on the hunky UPS guy who delivers packages to the salon.

As I giggled while Elle taught Paulette a man-catching move in the film's now-iconic "bend and snap" scene, I couldn't help but wonder: *Where had I* seen *this actor before?* Something about her unique voice, her funny facial expressions, and her commitment to every line and bit. Oh my god, I soon realized, that's Sherri Ann Cabot! And she's also Stifler's Mom!

And just like that, my obsession with Jennifer Coolidge took root. Through the years I sought her out in *everything*: a rerun of *Seinfeld*, which was her very first onscreen appearance, where she played Jerry's masseuse girlfriend who refuses to give Jerry a massage; quirky indies like *Gentlemen Broncos*, where she acted with writer/director Mike White, a relationship that would change her career and life; and more mainstream fare, like the sweet holiday comedy *Single All the Way*—was there ever a more memorable Christmas pageant? And when she stepped off the boat in the first episode of *The White Lotus* as the filthy-rich and extremely complex Tanya McQuoid, I was hooked. And I wasn't alone.

What *is* it about Jennifer Coolidge that we all adore? E. Alex Jung, who profiled Jen for *Vulture*, may have said it best: "Part of her uniqueness is her mien, her lips that pout like a scrunchie, her hooded eyes, but really it's her voice and delivery that inspire delirium. The shortest lines—'Hi' or 'Okay' or 'So moist'—are putty in her hands. She stretches vowels out across entire emotional vistas: plaintive, alien, funny."

Jennifer Coolidge's career spans three decades. As of this writing, she has 131 acting credits on IMDb (the Internet Movie Database), and she's come a long way from her small Massachusetts hometown. Her versatile roles in film and television—from bit parts to leads, from memorable guest spots to recurring roles—include not only fantastic comedies but also serious dramas (*Promising Young Woman*) and fun voice-over gigs (*Robots, King of the Hill*), plus action adventures (*Shotgun Wedding*). Says podcaster and fellow Coolidge fanatic Evan Ross Katz: "She is an actress whose résumé is both lengthy and girthy, comprising a breadth of roles that in any other hands might not have cemented themselves in film history."

But most of all, Jennifer Coolidge is *relatable*. She's dealt with her share of rejections, setbacks, and heartbreak, but she's persevered and come out wiser, funnier, and more fabulous than ever. Most recently Jen won an Emmy® and a Golden Globe®, walked the red carpet at the Academy Awards®, and made a surprise appearance with the GLAAD Awards®. "These gays," as Jennifer observed in a nod to *The White Lotus* and to the crowd's delight, were *not* trying to murder her! If I loved her before, I absolutely heart her now.

This book is a celebration of everyone's favorite pop culture icon, Jennifer Coolidge, along with a look at her most memorable roles—and the ones you may *not* be as familiar with. Jennifer is five feet, ten inches of pure happiness—an animal lover, loyal friend, style icon, and screen legend—and in her sixties, but just getting started. More than anything, Jennifer Coolidge is a testament to the power of being your own hilarious, awesome self. The world would be a happier, quirkier, and cooler place if we could all be a little more like Jen.

# Early Life

Jennifer Audrey Coolidge was born on August 28, 1961, in Boston, Massachusetts, to Gretchen (née Knauff) and Paul Constant Coolidge. According to a profile in *Vulture* and *New York Magazine*, her father worked in resin manufacturing and was a craftsman on the side; her mother was a homemaker. She has two sisters, Elizabeth and Susannah, and one brother, Andrew. Jennifer was raised Unitarian Universalist, she told E. Alex Jung of *Vulture* as the two discussed reincarnation, "which," he said, "ultimately means she believes in some big-picture thinker in the sky, although she's not sure exactly what."

Jennifer's parents had a happy marriage, she recalls in the Jung profile. "My father really worshipped my mother. . . . He really thought she was the most incredible person that ever lived on this planet." The Coolidge family resided in Norwell, Massachusetts, a small town outside Boston, and Jennifer dreamed of being both a singer and an instrumental musician; she went to orchestra camp for three summers, playing the clarinet.

What was young Jennifer Coolidge like? "I was kind of out to lunch, to be honest," Jennifer told *The Times* podcast in 2022. "I was always sort of, like, off in my head and staring out the window or not listening to what anyone was saying. I was sort of inside my own mind."

Though Jennifer's parents always loved her, they worried she wouldn't have much of a chance at success, according to conversations she overheard as a child. "My bedroom was not far from the kitchen," she recalled on *The Times* podcast. "I could hear my parents talking about me and they were just like, 'Oh my God, what are we going to do? . . . What's going to become of her?'"

She was also a fast runner, admitting to *The Times* podcast, "That's the only other good thing I had going for me." Though Jennifer never looked at track and field as a career path, she always assumed she'd keep up that skill—and had a rude awakening decades later on set. "I did a movie recently, *Shotgun Wedding*, where you had to run really fast," Jennifer told *Vulture* in 2021. "I used to be a really, really fast runner, and I just assumed I still was. . . . This fantasy I had about myself, I thought I was an Olympic athlete, you know? . . . It was a humbling moment."

Not only was Jennifer fast, but from a very young age, her creativity shone bright. In second grade Jennifer won "a contest for who could name the six guinea pigs in the classroom," she told *Us Weekly*. "I named one Bell Bottoms. I can't believe they went for it." That same teacher, Jennifer continued, asked the students "to write a flattering paragraph about our moms for Mother's Day." The first line of Jennifer's paragraph: "My mother has soft brown eyes like a cow."

Jennifer is a lifelong film fan. As she grew older, she told *Us Weekly*, "I begged teachers to let me substitute movies for papers." And at ten years old she took a shot at making her own movie—a reboot of the classic film *Jaws*. "My dad swam with a fin on his back and my sister was the shark victim," she remembered. The next year, Jennifer said to *Us Weekly*, she gave her acting skills a try offstage: "I bought a case of beer when I was 11, with my mother's wig."

As Jennifer grew older, she received advice from her father that she would always remember and later apply to her career and life. "My father used to always say to me—he said it more than any other little phrase—'Jennifer, you have to remember that character is fate,'" she told *Deadline* in 2022. "And I think he's right. Who you are forms your ending, and you have the power to be good or rotten."

Jennifer attended both Norwell High School and the Cambridge School of Weston. She earned her bachelor's degree in theater from Boston's Emerson College in 1985. Her high school yearbook quote would prove to be telling: "There is no sacrifice too great for man's art."

# Making It

"I was kind of a lost soul for a really long time," Jennifer shared with comedian and podcaster Marc Maron in 2017. After college Jennifer moved to Los Angeles for the first time. Because her father would help financially if she was in school, Jennifer studied at the American Academy of Dramatic Arts and lived in some interesting places, including a room in a nursing home and a beachside house with a unique roommate.

"I was dating this guy, and his brother's parrot was loose in his apartment," Jennifer said of one of these places, a house in Venice Beach, where she and her then-boyfriend also waited tables. "It didn't matter where you were in the apartment, it would eventually just fly over you and dump on you." Eventually Jennifer got tired of both the boyfriend and the parrot, so she returned to the East Coast.

As a young twentysomething in Manhattan, Jennifer went on auditions and dabbled in the sketch comedy scene. She also worked as a cocktail waitress at a restaurant called Canals, alongside a then-unknown actress named Sandra Bullock, who was a hostess. However, Jennifer told Maron, the two women treated their acting careers very differently.

"She was actually doing the life," said Jennifer of Bullock. After their nightly shift ended at 2:00 a.m., Bullock would go home and prepare for auditions, while Jennifer embraced New York nightlife with a vengeance. Before long, Jennifer developed a problem with cocaine. "And one time my sister said, I went to visit her down in New Orleans, and she was like, 'Oh my god, Jennifer, your head is too big for your body,'" she told Maron. After that, with the support of her family, Jennifer entered a rehab facility at twenty-seven years old and graduated.

In 1990 a slightly older, wiser, and recovered Jennifer returned to Los Angeles, but this time she had a plan. Knowing that a curriculum would keep her focused, she began classes at The Groundlings, an iconic improv troupe whose alumni include the likes of Will Ferrell, Lisa Kudrow, and Melissa McCarthy. Though Jennifer had a lot to learn—"You have to be able to come up with some sort of activity while you're talking to someone, and for the first two years I was on a golf course [or] I would be stirring a bowl of batter with a spoon," she confessed to Maron—she eventually made an impression, first joining the Sunday performance company, then The Groundlings' main company.

Jennifer's secret? Pretending to be people she knew and didn't like. She told Maron: "I don't think I was a great writer, but . . . I had a really good ear for exactly what someone said to me. And I always had these really condescending bosses, and I could remember exactly their wording and everything. So, I would just write it all down immediately. And then just put it on stage. . . . I got out all of my anger and everything by just recreating these, you know, people that made my life difficult."

# Be More Like Jen: Top Six Life Lessons from Our Queen

Jennifer Coolidge's life hasn't been all fabulous gowns and gold statuettes. She's kicked substance abuse in the butt, experienced heartbreak, and endured many career ups and downs. Nevertheless, she persisted: finding (and keeping) friends who love and support her, seeking out the place where she feels most at home, and, most of all, becoming her own authentic self. Here are the top six life lessons we can all learn from the one, the only, the divine Ms. Coolidge.

## 1 NEVER GIVE UP ON YOUR DREAMS, EVEN WHEN IT'S HARD

Jennifer got her big break—her guest spot on *Seinfeld*—when she was thirty-two years old. By then she'd been trying to "make it" for over a decade: taking acting and improv classes, going on endless auditions, and working thankless jobs. Jen bounced from Boston to LA to New York and back to LA again and overcame addiction along the way. Shortly after Jennifer booked the *Seinfeld* role, she lost her mother to cancer.

Not everyone appreciated Jennifer's tall blonde voluptuousness, especially early on. Jennifer told E. Alex Jung of *Vulture* that an LA roommate said to her, "I don't see you as someone in front of the camera." During the same period a casting agent called Jennifer for a meeting and promptly told Jennifer she'd never cast her in anything because "I only cast good-looking people on my soaps."

Even once Jennifer embarked on an acting career, not all her projects were hits—far from it. The same day she got *Seinfeld*, Jennifer also booked a sketch comedy show called *SheTV* that ABC quickly canceled. Another sketch show, Fox's *Saturday Night Special*, met the same fate, despite having Kathy Griffin as another cast member and Roseanne Barr as a producer. Earlier on, Jennifer experienced a major blow to her comedy career—a lost chance to join the cast of NBC's iconic *Saturday Night Live*.

Jennifer shared that experience with comedian and podcaster Marc Maron in 2017. In the early 1990s she and a group of other Groundlings members, including Will Ferrell, Cheri Oteri, and Chris Kattan (Jennifer dated Kattan and still thinks of him fondly), were flown to New York to audition for *SNL*. The audition went well, and upon returning to Los Angeles, the actors were "put on hold" for three months while casting decisions were made. Though this isn't an uncommon industry practice, Jennifer's new agent felt the hold was an insult. "[H]e was like, 'I think that's outrageous,'" Jennifer recalled. "'And I'm gonna tell them that they either make up their mind today or . . . we're not doing it.'"

Did the *SNL* ultimatum work out? No, and neither did the agent. Soon after, Jennifer told Maron, she called her agent's office, only to be informed that he'd quit and gone to work for his family's meat business! While Jennifer admitted that she'd treat the situation very differently today—probably letting *SNL* know directly that she'd had an issue with her agent but was still available—she was still fairly new to the industry, and thus her *Saturday Night Live* dreams were dashed.

Even after the successes of *Legally Blonde* and a string of Christopher Guest films, Jennifer continued to experience setbacks. She lost the role of Lynette on *Desperate Housewives*. Not all her films and TV shows were hits. Still, Jennifer persevered, eventually landing regular television roles, branching out into theater and voice-over, and sticking with films before becoming the Emmy®-winning legend we know and love today.

For every role Jennifer got, there were many, many more she didn't. At a particularly dark time in her twenties, her penchant for drugs and partying threatened any career plans. And her growing success as a character actress didn't mean there wouldn't be more failures along the way.

However, Jennifer always kept going. She went to rehab and moved back to Los Angeles, where she knew she could take classes, make contacts, and go for the gigs she wanted. Even after the *Saturday Night Live* debacle, when many would have given up, Jennifer kept performing with The Groundlings and was eventually discovered by Catherine O'Hara and Christopher Guest, whom she'd work with in multiple films, including the career-defining *Best in Show*.

Jennifer never gave up on her dreams, even when addiction, lost opportunities, and box-office flops threatened to stand in her way.

Whether you're an actor, an artist, or a truck driver, take a page from The Book of Jennifer Coolidge today, and *never give up.*

## 2 | GO BIG OR GO HOME

You *always* remember Jennifer Coolidge! Even her TV guest roles are incredibly memorable. Is it her distinctive voice? Is it her fantastic facial expressions? Her incredible physical delivery?

Or is it *all of the above*?

Lead part, guest spot, three lines or three hundred—it doesn't matter: Jennifer Coolidge commits to the role and commits *big*. Even in more serious fare, Jennifer brings humor to the smallest moment, and you never forget a Jennifer Coolidge character. *Ever.*

Jen commits big in her personal life as well, going on over two hundred dates after her popularity in *American Pie*, purchasing a historic home in New Orleans, and moving to LA not once but twice to act. She brought her signature style to everything from *Sex and the City* to *2 Broke Girls* to *Shotgun Wedding*—even wielding an assault rifle and screaming, "Nobody fucks with my family!"

On the awards show circuit, Jen is no shrinking violet: she wears gorgeous dresses on red carpets and isn't afraid to sport high heels that make her even taller. And when Jennifer won a Golden Globe Award® in 2023 for *The White Lotus* (she rocked a black Dolce & Gabbana sequined dress and a stunning blonde sixties-style bouffant and was escorted onstage by hunky Colin Farrell while giving him an eyeful of appreciation), her speech was positively *epic*. Here's a highlight:

*I just want you all to know that I had such big dreams and expectations as a younger person, but what happened is they get sort of fizzled out by life and whatever. . . . I had these giant ideas. And then you get older, and, oh, shit's going to happen. And Mike White, you have given me hope. You've given me a new beginning . . . even if this is the end because you killed me off. But even if this is the end, you changed my life in a million different ways.*

White Lotus creator and Jennifer's close friend White was moved to tears, and can you blame him? The entire speech was vulnerable, lovely, and uniquely hilarious, and Jennifer paid tribute to White and those who had given her opportunities along the way—Ryan Murphy (*The Watcher*), Reese Witherspoon (*Legally Blonde*), Michael Patrick King

(*2 Broke Girls*), and Paul and Chris Weitz (*American Pie*). Acceptance speeches can feel cliché, overlong, and dull, but not with Jennifer, who went straight for the heart and made us love her even more.

Jennifer also made a grand surprise entrance at the 2023 GLAAD Awards®, voicing her support for the LGBTQIA+ community: "We all have a right to be who we are and to love the people that we love and tell our stories and celebrate that in every way that we can," she said. Jennifer was then given her own surprise: GLAAD's Special Recognition Award, presented by her *Best in Show* costar and longtime friend, Jane Lynch.

Most of us aren't living that red-carpet life, wearing top-name designers, or making our living in front of a camera, but we *can* take a page from Jennifer's book: go big or go home.

## 3 ) TRY EVERYTHING— DON'T PUT YOURSELF IN A BOX

Over more than three decades, Jennifer has done it *all*. As a film actress, she's performed broad comedy (*American Pie, Legally Blonde*), subtle and improvisation-heavy (the Christopher Guest oeuvre, most notably *Best in Show*), action-camp (*Shotgun Wedding*), and dark revenge fantasy (*Promising Young Woman*). On television she's been a daffy but resolute masseuse (*Seinfeld*), a compassionate lady of the night (*The Secret Life of the American Teenager*), a delightfully conniving real estate agent (*The Watcher*), and a grieving daughter of endless wealth in the most luxe locations (*The White Lotus*). Giving new meaning to the term *character actress,* Jennifer's forever workin' it, voicing a gassy but loving automaton (*Robots*), playing the ultimate LA power agent (*Joey*), and directing a Christmas pageant with small-town flair (*Single All the Way*).

And that's not all! Jennifer has toured as a stand-up comedian and appeared not once but *twice* on the Great White Way—in the Broadway revival of Clare Booth Luce's iconic play *The Women* (2001–2002) and the 2010 play *Elling,* alongside Brendan Fraser and Denis O'Hare.

What can we learn from this? Simple: it's never too late to break out of your comfort zone and try something new. We've all been in a rut more than once or felt stuck in a specific job, domestic role, or even personality type. Take a cue from Jennifer Coolidge's impressive résumé, and put yourself out there.

Change can be scary: it's never easy to try a new hobby, make a career change, or do *anything* outside of the daily routine all of us become accustomed to, especially the older we get. Staying inside a box, though comforting, can also be stifling. In Jennifer's case, scripted comedy differs from improv, which differs from drama, which differs from action, and *all* of these differ greatly from live performance, whether that's infusing new energy into the same dialogue you recite night after night or taking the mic as a stand-up comic.

Even though she doesn't have a one-hour stand-up special as of this book's publication—but never say never—Jennifer even gave stand-up a go and lived to tell the tale. If she can tell jokes at clubs, you can take a trapeze class or order a new coffee drink, right? Do it for Jen.

## ◀ KEEP YOUR FRIENDS CLOSE . . . THAT'S IT

Jen surrounds herself with friends and family. Her sister, Susannah, is also her neighbor in New Orleans. Acclaimed actress Naomi Watts, Jennifer's costar on *The Watcher,* helped Jen find a gorgeous New York City apartment while they were filming, and Jennifer let director Sofia Coppola film 2017's *The Beguiled* at her own NOLA home. Jane Lynch, who played Christy Cummings in *Best in Show,* values Jen as a long-time friend and collaborator. Said Jane of Jennifer at the 2023 GLAAD Awards®: "I love you, sweetie. . . . This wonderful woman here was pro-gay before it was cool to be pro-gay. She is one of us, ladies and [gentle-men]. And I have always said that the world has to catch up to Jennifer Coolidge. And the world has caught up to Jennifer Coolidge!"

Ryan Murphy filmed a scene from *American Horror Story: Coven* at Jennifer's New Orleans house, and he later cast her as Whitney S. Pierce on *Glee* and as Karen Calhoun in *The Watcher.* Jennifer was thrilled at this fruitful connection. "I remember thinking, 'Maybe I can go out in the yard and bump into Ryan, and he could give me a part in this,'" Jennifer told *Vogue.* "For it to happen ten years later, it feels just as good."

But the biggest life lesson on keeping your friends close can be found in Jennifer's unique and powerful relationship with *White Lotus* creator, actor, and *Survivor* runner-up, Mike White.

"[T]here are these friends that don't let you go. That's Mike White," Jennifer told *The Ringer* in 2021. She said to *Vogue* in 2022: "Mike was that person in the world that you hope exists. That person that gives you a challenge that makes a difference in your life."

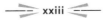

Jennifer never hesitates to sing White's praises. She's called him a "genius" in various interviews and gave him a heartfelt, tearful thank-you in her Golden Globes® acceptance speech for season two of *The White Lotus* (see page xx to read what she said). But their relationship goes deeper than that single collaboration.

Jennifer and Mike met on the set of 2009's *Gentlemen Broncos* when Mike played Dusty, the love interest of Jennifer's character, Judith Purvis. After filming wrapped, the two stayed in touch, and when Mike's partner couldn't go on an African safari the two had planned, Mike invited Jennifer. "We slept in tents in the Serengeti," Jennifer told *Us Weekly*. "I would search the tent for hours looking for snakes [but] never saw one."

While on safari Mike witnessed Jennifer's quirks in full force. "[S]he'd be like, 'Oh, there's a leopard!' And then she'd be like, 'The leopard is looking at us weird,'" Mike told *Vulture* in 2021. "[S]he would go from loving the beauty of nature to projecting on this animal that they want to eat us, and we've got to get the fuck out of there."

Mike wanted to give Jennifer a gift: a full, nuanced character who wasn't the butt of every joke. First, he wrote a road-trip comedy for her called *The Clouds of St. Patsy*, in which Jennifer would have played a paranoid actress journeying to an obscure film festival she's increasingly certain is a ruse planted by her ex. HBO passed on the show, but during the pandemic they commissioned Mike for a project with a quick turnaround—a limited series that could be made safely in quarantine. Mike said yes, but only if Jennifer could have a major role. HBO agreed.

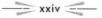

Spoiler alert: initially Jennifer didn't *want* to play Tanya McQuoid, a role Mike wrote just for her. Jennifer was isolating at her NOLA home, eating vegan pizzas with her assistant, when Mike called and offered her the role. "I was like, 'I'm not doing that. I'm not going to Hawaii,'" Jennifer recalled on *The Times* podcast. "I'm out of shape . . . and not mentally in shape for a job." Both Mike and a friend of Jennifer's from her Groundlings days urged her to reconsider, and soon Jennifer was on her way to Hawaii to shoot *The White Lotus*.

Jennifer made even more friends while filming. Because of the pandemic, cast and crew all stayed at the Four Seasons Maui, where the show was shot. They ate meals together, and according to Jennifer, many would swim in the ocean after shooting wrapped for the day or night. "Everyone sort of bonded together," Jennifer told *The Ringer* in 2021. "We were doing this scary thing and shooting during COVID, but even though it was incredibly difficult, with the heat and all of that, there was something kind of magical about it going on, I can't explain."

*The White Lotus* was a massive success. Originally written as a six-part limited series, it was renewed by HBO for a second season, and Mike made the decision to set it in a new exotic location—this time, Sicily. And when Tanya McQuoid exited the boat and informed beleaguered manager Valentina (Sabrina Impacciatore) of her new Blossom Circle client status, viewers squealed, and awards juries took notice.

At the 2023 Golden Globes® Jennifer thanked a tearful Mike for his love and support. They even reunited for a set of hilarious ads for e.l.f. Cosmetics, the first of which debuted during the 2023 Super Bowl. And although Tanya won't be in season three, Jennifer and Mike are still tight. "He's just really exceptional," Jennifer said to *The Ringer*. "One in a billion."

## 5⟩ FIND YOUR TRUE HOME

Jennifer's love of New Orleans began when her sister, Susannah, attended Tulane University and Jennifer would visit. Over the years Jennifer visited NOLA—and visited often. "I was just blown away. . . . It's sort of this undiscovered secret," she told Marc Maron in 2017. "I really fell in love with it and became obsessed with it. And every time I had a break on a job, I would go down there and just hang out. Look at real estate."

Once Jennifer had the means as a successful actor, she found a beautiful old house in NOLA's Lower Garden District and now considers NOLA her home. Jennifer welcomed *Vulture* writer E. Alex Jung into her house in 2021. Here's what Jung had to say about the experience:

> *She bought this 1867 house just before Hurricane Katrina and has spent much of her time restoring it to its former Greek Revival–slash–Italianate glory: shoring up the foundation, replacing the wiring, repairing the roof, patching the plaster, and filling it with Persian rugs, tasseled ottomans, an upholstered minibar, armoires. Oil portraits in gilded frames stare down from the high walls. Coolidge believes there is a "presence" in the house, although not an evil one.*

Jennifer relishes being a hostess. At one point, she told Marc Maron in 2017, she threw an impromptu dinner party on a Monday night, something she said would never happen in Los Angeles. Each Halloween, she told Jung, she hosts an elaborate party in the house, complete with onsite entertainment (including burlesque dancers) and enough food and wine to keep revelers reveling. And occasionally there's a required costume.

"She's fascinated by liars and con men," Jung writes. "The last time she had a Halloween party, in 2019, the costume prompt was to dress up as your favorite narcissist—or their victim; this year, she's thinking it will be to come as your favorite fraud. These themes may or may not be inspired by personal experience."

Jennifer has made herself at home in the Big Easy. She loves the restaurant Saint-Germain, where they always remember her preference for French wine. According to Jung's profile, Jennifer's friend Mason Hereford runs one of her favorite restaurants, called Molly's Rise and Shine. When Hereford opened the restaurant, Jennifer bought hundreds of dollars' worth of gift cards, and when she hired him to cater a party, she paid double his going rate.

Through her NOLA home, Jennifer demonstrates the importance of finding the place where each of us can be the most *ourselves*. In New Orleans, a city known for its vibrant history, its unique culture, and its diverse population, Jennifer experiences much-needed respite from the hustle and bustle of Hollywood as well as the unpredictable schedules of movie and TV sets. She can dress up in the flamboyant outfits she loves—such as "a silk cheetah-print caftan and crystal encrusted heels" or "a black slip and a sheer fuchsia-and-gold bolero," Jung writes—without second looks or judgment. She can bond with family and friends, whether it's over intimate dinners at her fave places, spontaneous Monday-night gatherings, or her annual Halloween blowout.

For Jennifer, "home" is more than just where she lays her head at night. It's people she cares about, the small pleasures, and the place where she can be fully and completely herself. That's a life lesson we all can take away: Where do you feel your best, and how can you spend as much time as possible there?

## 6 ) ABOVE ALL, BE YOUR HILARIOUS, QUIRKY, AWESOME SELF!

Jennifer Coolidge is truly one of a kind. She was already a successful working actor when she met Mike White. However, as they developed a friendship and eventually went on safari together, White saw how truly fabulous she was—and set out to give her life-changing opportunities so the whole world could see too.

Since then, Jennifer has been on a whirlwind rise. She's winning awards, appearing in ads for Old Navy, and even booking a campaign for e.l.f. Cosmetics. She's made surprise appearances at awards shows, was honored by *TIME* magazine *and* PETA, and is greeted with open arms and gigantic laughs everywhere she goes. All by being just who she is.

Jennifer has never fit the mold of a typical Hollywood starlet—and that's okay. She's made a sparkling career *and* a happy life. Jennifer doesn't need a script to be hilarious: she got her start making up characters at The Groundlings, and her iconic "eulogy" in *The White Lotus* was mainly improvised. She's proudly quirky, loving her dogs, her historic home, and the city that surrounds it, and entertaining her friends, whether that's at a spur-of-the-moment dinner party or a lavish Halloween bash. Most of all, Jennifer is awesome: she's experienced considerable struggles and come out swinging, and everything—from career to home to personal life—is just getting better and better.

The biggest life lesson we can take from Jennifer Coolidge can be summed up in two simple words: *be yourself*. Whatever that means to you—eschewing a traditional career or family structure, making the home of your dreams, breaking free from your comfort zone, or even adopting a new pet—you too can live the life you want if you embrace exactly who you are. Life isn't always easy, whether you're an up-and-coming performer, someone working in a cubicle, or someone just trying to figure it out. However, if you dig deep within yourself and realize just what makes you special, life can be a wonderful journey, just as it has been for Jennifer Coolidge.

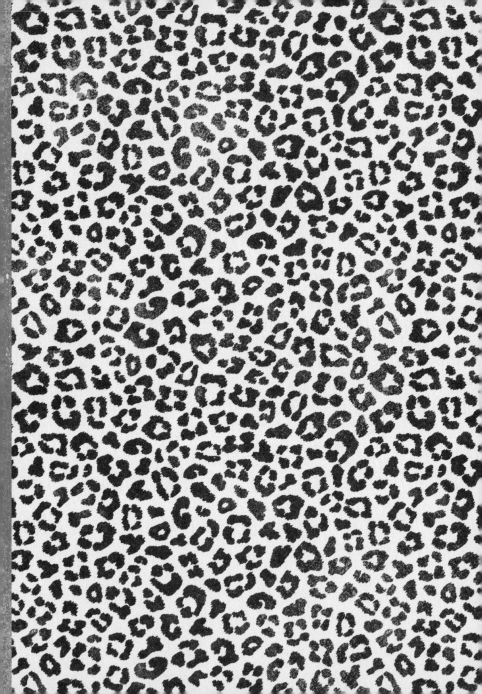

# Iconic Movie Roles

Over the past two decades Jennifer Coolidge has made a big impression on the silver screen. From a Scotch-swilling seductress to a dim-bulb trophy wife, to a sweet manicurist with a crush, she's played every type—and that's just in the early 2000s. Jen has worked with legends like Fred Willard (*Best in Show*, *A Mighty Wind*), Carey Mulligan (*Promising Young Woman*), and Reese Witherspoon (*Legally Blonde*), and she added drama and animation films to her arsenal of awesomeness. Here's a highlight reel of Jen's movie magic.

# Jeanine Stifler
## *(aka Stifler's Mom)*
### *American Pie* (1999)

---

**NOTABLE QUOTABLES**

*"I got some scotch. Aged eighteen years—the way I like it."*

------------

*"Mister Finch, are you trying to seduce me?"*

---

Blonde hair, tight frock, long legs: Jeanine Stifler is a temptress, pure and simple. In the original *American Pie*—a movie responsible for bringing the raunchy teen sex comedy to a whole new generation—Stifler's Mom is a mere myth whose sexy photo is circulated at parties attended by her son, loud and insensitive teenage womanizer Steve Stifler (Seann William Scott), and his four frenemies led by Jim (Jason Biggs), who have made a pact to lose their virginity by the end of senior year. Seeing the picture of Stifler's Mom, a classmate (John Cho) proclaims: "She's a MILF—a mom I'd like to fuck!" (Yes, the character who arguably put the term "MILF" on the map and launched it into the zeitgeist was played by none other than Jennifer Coolidge!)

It's not until prom night—when Jim and his friends are down to the sex-pact wire—that the legend herself makes an appearance, offering a drink to Jim's bestie, Finch (Eddie Kaye Thomas). When Finch refers to her as "quite striking," that seals the deal, and the wild sexcapades

ensue. (In case you were worried, he's eighteen.) Meanwhile, Jeanine's son—known only as "Stifler" and who has been harassing Jim, Finch, and their pals about their virginity for the whole film—accidentally peeks in and witnesses the shenanigans. He is rightfully *horrified*, but you know what they say about karma.

Thanks to Stifler's Mom, Finch's virginity is a thing of the past, but as the boys grow into men, he may not have seen the last of her . . .

## *Why We Heart Stifler's Mom*

Let's just say the song "Devil with a Blue Dress On" could have been written about both Jeanine Stifler *and* Jennifer Coolidge. No matter how you feel about *American Pie*, we must love the movie that propelled Jennifer Coolidge into the big time. Here she's a tall, blonde hottie who knows exactly what she wants—Scotch and a younger man—and how to get it, while paraphrasing the classic film *The Graduate*.

As Stifler's Mom, Jennifer is striking and powerful, ensuring a life-long place in the iconic teen movie canon as she wields a crystal tumbler and seduces her son's friend. And she looks absolutely stunning in blue to boot. After this film Jennifer went on to star in many more, but we'll never, ever forget Stifler's Mom—because as Jennifer Coolidge showed us all, funny can be *sexy* too.

## FUN BONUS FACTS

✳ Jennifer reprised her role as Stifler's Mom in this film's sequels *American Pie 2* (2001), *American Wedding* (2003), and *American Reunion* (2012).

✳ Jennifer's role as Stifler's Mom in *American Pie* was good for more than just her bank account. Jennifer told *Variety*, "I got a lot of play at being a MILF and I got a lot of sexual action from *American Pie*. . . . There were so many benefits to doing that movie. I mean, there would be like 200 people that I would never have slept with."

# Sherri Ann Cabot

## *Best in Show* (2000)

---

### NOTABLE QUOTABLES

*"Leslie and I have an amazing relationship and it's very physical—he still pushes all my buttons. People say, 'Oh, but he's so much older than you,' and you know what, I'm the one having to push him away. We have so much in common—we both love soup and snow peas, we love the outdoors, and talking and not talking. We could not talk or talk forever and still find things to not talk about."*

------------

*[about a poodle's furballs] "Those act as flippers."*

---

Big blonde hair, flashy clothing, a vacant look in her heavily made-up eyes, and plenty o'bling: Sherri Ann Cabot could win an Oscar for Best Trophy Wife. She lives in a mansion outside Philadelphia with her husband of five years, Leslie Ward Cabot (Patrick Crenshaw), who is significantly older than Sherri Ann. But don't worry—their relationship is so physical, *she's* the one having to push *him* away. Plus, they both love soup and snow peas, so it's a match made in heaven.

Sherri Ann is also perfectly matched with Christy Cummings (Jane Lynch), the short-haired dog lover and handler of Sherri Ann's own dog. Nicknamed "Butch" (for . . . reasons), Rhapsody in White is a gorgeous standard poodle and two-time Best in Show winner of the annual

Mayflower Kennel Club Dog Show. "I wanted the best handler, and I get what I want!" Sherri Ann proclaims. And Christy benefits too, in more ways than one (*wink wink, nudge nudge*).

Thanks to the Cabots' generosity, Christy's own dog kennel has been completely transformed from a "shitbox"—Sherri Ann's words—to a cutting-edge facility where pooches receive exactly what they need. Speaking of needs, while Sherri Ann already has a spouse, she and Christy have a family dynamic all their own. Christy is the taskmaster and disciplinarian, while Sherri Ann provides the unconditional love and special decorative touches.

Because Rhapsody in White is a two-time winner, the poodle appears on local television before the big show, accompanied by an always-enthused Christy and a freshly blown-out, tight-power-suit-

sporting, cleavage-pushed-to-the-heavens Sherri Ann. "Butch is a bitch!" Christy informs the hosts while showing them the fluffy fur pom-poms that keep the dog's hips warm.

Later that night is the very exclusive preshow party at the Cabot mansion, which officially ends when the ice sculpture of Butch melts. Sherri Ann and Butch sport matching tiaras, and both charm Mayflower Kennel Club president Dr. Theodore Millbank (Bob Balaban), while Christy tries to curry favor with Dr. Millbank for a third Best in Show, and the perpetually silent Leslie holds court in a tuxedo.

Sherri Ann and Christy are especially excited because this year Sherri Ann will be doing Christy's makeup for the big show. To quote Sherri Ann, "It's a way for me to relax, and it's also a way to show, again, my art." Christy considers Sherri Ann "the epitome of glamour," and Sherri Ann thinks Christy could use a little herself.

On the day of the show Sherri Ann and Christy congregate backstage with the rest of the barking hopefuls and their owners. Unfortunately, Christy's makeover did not quite pan out. Sherri Ann tells the camera, "I did a wonderful Sophia Loren Persian eye, and it looked very dramatic, and it was very show-like." Christy begs to differ: "It was over the top, and I looked freakish," but she concedes, "I do like what she did with my hair," earning a smile from Sherri Ann.

While Christy is at full confidence—she even tries to psych out competitor Harlan Pepper (Christopher Guest) and his prized bloodhound, Hubert, to no avail—Sherri Ann is a bundle of nerves. While Christy readies herself to handle Rhapsody in White in the ring, Sherri Ann patronizes the concession stand, ordering an extra-large popcorn, half butter, half salt. "My nervousness is rubbing off on Leslie," Sherri Ann confides, munching away. "I feel like I really need to listen to my inner instinct, and my inner instinct is saying, don't go right now. So, I'm not going out. I'm gonna be right here until I get another message, from myself."

After Rhapsody in White triumphs in the first round, winning first place in the nonsporting group and advancing to Best in Show, Sherri Ann's inner message is clear. She and Christy—clad in a black suit with white piping that inspires the comment "She looks like a cocktail waitress on an oil rig" from Shih Tzu owner/handler Scott (John Michael Higgins)—share a big hug and then a passionate kiss! Watching the make-out on television with his partner Stefan (Michael McKean), Scott remarks, "Rhapsody has two mommies."

Will Rhapsody in White win a third Best in Show? Sadly, no. Christy is visibly *shocked* when Butch is overlooked in favor of Winky, the adorable Norwich terrier handled by owner Gerry Fleck (Eugene Levy), who triumphs despite having, literally, two left feet. However, the story hasn't ended for Sherri Ann and Christy.

Six months later the owner and her handler are officially a couple. Not only that, but they've also embarked upon a new business venture: *American Bitch*, a magazine that focuses on "the issues of the lesbian purebred dog owner," Christy proudly states. Even though Sherri Ann expresses her sadness at Rhapsody in White's non-win—"it was so not right"—she is happily in love with Ms. Cummings. "Sherri Ann is definitely the inspiration [for *American Bitch*]. . . . She has a very big heart, she's generous, she's kind, she's sweet," Christy gushes. "Well, vicea-versa," Sherri responds. "She's changed my life, and as it turns out, she's dynamite in the sack," Christy exclaims. How else can Sherri Ann respond but, "Likewise, I'm sure."

And they all lived doggily ever after!

## Why We Heart Sherri Ann

Not all media ages well, but *Best in Show* holds up over two decades later. Collectively and individually, the ensemble cast is nothing short of comedic genius. And Jennifer Coolidge is a major part of that.

Sherri Ann Cabot has an integral role in this quirky group of dog owners—from earnest fisherman Harlan Pepper to feuding suburbanite lawyers Hamilton and Meg Swan (Michael Hitchcock and Parker Posey), who impose their neuroses on their poor Weimaraner, Beatrice, to Gerry Fleck and his formerly promiscuous wife, Cookie (Catherine O'Hara), who love making up songs about their favorite breed: terriers.

Maybe Sherri Ann isn't the brightest bulb, but she always looks fantastic, whether she's rocking a pink puffy coat and white marabou headband while frolicking with Christy's dogs or sporting a royal purple suit at the Mayflower Kennel Club show. She has genuine affection for both husband and handler as well as her beautiful purebred dog. And when she kisses Christy on national television, it's obvious she's ready to move into the next phase of her life: girlfriend and lesbian dog owner magazine magnate.

When she accepted the role in *Best in Show*, Jennifer signed on to a very unconventional filmmaking process. And being Jen, she completely rose to the occasion. Beginning with *Waiting for Guffman* and

continuing the tradition of cult favorite *This Is Spinal Tap*, Christopher Guest's mockumentaries assemble the best and brightest of comedic actors highly skilled at improvisation, who present their individual obsessions, from catalogs to fake fur, as completely normal—and to these characters, they are. By design, the "scripts" for these movies are very short (*Best in Show*'s script was only sixteen pages long), and the rest of it is up to the cast. It's no wonder Jennifer Coolidge fit right in.

According to interviews, Catherine O'Hara introduced Jennifer to Guest after both saw Jennifer perform with The Groundlings. Though she'd already made a memorable appearance in *American Pie*, Jennifer's gift for improv—not just making up dialogue but also creating an entire character, from voice to mannerisms to how they react to every place, situation, and person—is on full display in *Best in Show*. Jennifer spouts memorable lines with a toss of her pretty blonde head, munches popcorn with the nerves that only a budding lesbian dog owner can have, and follows her heart wherever it goes—in this case, right into the arms of her dog handler. Eugene Levy—*Schitt's Creek* actor and Guest's writing partner, who also had a pivotal parental role in the *American Pie* films—said to *New York Magazine*: "[Jennifer] is her own comedic universe in and out of character."

## FUN BONUS FACTS

✴ *Best in Show* was the first of four films Jennifer would do with director Christopher Guest. The other three are *A Mighty Wind* (2003), *For Your Consideration* (2006), and *Mascots* (2016). This is no accident: "Jennifer is amazing at playing off of people," Guest told *New York Magazine*. "And if there isn't someone to play off of, then she plays off the silence."

✴ Jennifer based Sherri Ann on a "very feminine, very phony" woman she worked for in Los Angeles.

✴ Jennifer and her costar Jane Lynch reunited on the red carpet of the 2023 GLAAD Awards®. The two posed for pictures and looked ecstatic to see one another. Of course, they both looked stunning. Too bad Jennifer didn't do Jane's makeup . . . this time, anyway.

# Paulette Bonafonté

*Legally Blonde* (2001) and
*Legally Blonde 2: Red, White & Blonde* (2003)

## NOTABLE QUOTABLES

*"What's a girl to do? He's a guy who followed his pecker to greener pastures, and I'm just a middle-aged high school dropout who's got stretch marks and a fat ass!"*

------------

*"I'm taking the dog, dumbass!"*

------------

*"You look like the Fourth of July. It makes me want a hot dog real bad."*

Elle Woods (Reese Witherspoon) is having the worst day *ever*. When her first class at Harvard Law School—a university that the California sorority girl only applied for to win back the love of her life, Warner Huntington III (Matthew Davis)—is cut short by *utter humiliation*, there's only one place to go in her cute convertible: the nearest nail salon. Manicures always make Elle feel better, and right now, it's an emergency. Salvation arrives in the form of a sad-Sally manicurist with frizzy hair, presently munching on a donut while reading a magazine story entitled "Are You Dying?" Ladies and gentlemen, Paulette Bonafonté has entered the chat.

"Bad day?" Paulette sympathetically asks a crying Elle, who nods. "Spill!" Paulette entreats, getting to work on her new client's nails after taking just *one* more bite of said donut. And just like that, a friendship— no, a blonde sisterhood—is born.

On the surface the two women seem very different. Elle is clad in head-to-toe designer gear, from her fitted green jacket to her sassy high-heeled boots, whereas Paulette is rocking plain denim and bright pink lipstick, with only a tiny bit of sparkle in her hair clips. Elle is chatty, but Paulette is quiet—until she finds herself opening up to the sweet sorority girl.

They trade sob stories: once the president of her sorority Delta Nu at California University Los Angeles, Elle blew off her final Greek week, hired a Coppola to direct her admission-essay video, and left her entire life behind to move to Cambridge, Massachusetts, to attend Harvard Law School (yes, that Harvard; yes, she got in—what, like it's hard?).

When she arrives on the East Coast, however, everyone is vile and unwelcoming. Terrifying Professor Stromwell (Holland Taylor) kicks Elle out of class for being unprepared. Worst of all, Warner is engaged to nasty Vivian Kensington (Selma Blair), who could use some mascara and serious highlights but is *not* completely unfortunate looking.

Paulette can listen and supply tissues but can't really help Elle, as she's in a pickle of her own. After all, she was recently kicked out by her boyfriend of eight years, Dewey—who kept both their trailer and her bull-dog, Rufus, before Paulette could even throw Rufus a birthday party. (As a devoted dog mom herself, Elle is shocked by Dewey's sheer audacity.)

As Elle soon sees, Paulette can't even keep it together enough to greet the hunky UPS guy (Bruce Thomas), who she has a major crush on. Poor Paulette fumbles around and spills nail solution when he looks *right her way*. However, after determining that "if a girl like you can't hold on to her man, there sure as hell isn't any hope for the rest of us," Paulette encourages Elle to "steal the bastard back!"

Unfortunately, Elle can't steal back said bastard—but maybe that's not so bad. After Vivian tricks Elle into coming to a non-costumed party dressed as a sexy bunny, and Warner condescendingly tells Elle, "You're just not smart enough, sweetie!" Elle decides to show everyone and pos-itively *crush* law school. But she doesn't forget Paulette, even bringing her law texts to the salon as the two of them—and Bruiser too—get their hair re-blonded side by side.

Always a good friend, Elle accompanies Paulette to the trailer where terrible Dewey still lives with Paulette's beloved pooch, Rufus. "What the hell do you want?" Dewey sneers at Paulette, who completely loses

her power around her ex. "You just thought you'd come here and show me what I'm definitely not missing?" he jeers. Clad in a mauve puffer jacket and a star-dotted turtleneck, topped off with an unfashionable scrunchie, Paulette clearly feels pathetic—and that will *not* happen on Elle's watch!

With less than a semester of law school under her belt, Elle spontaneously decides to pose as Paulette's attorney. Using legal jargon—sometimes even accurately!—Elle informs Dewey that Paulette is entitled to "full canine property ownership." When an utterly baffled Dewey asks, "Come again?" for the millionth time, Paulette translates: "I'm taking the dog, *dumbass!*"

As the ladies drive away, Paulette cuddles Rufus, and Paulette and Elle laugh at the befuddled, potbellied Dewey. "He's probably still scratching his head!" Elle giggles, to which Paulette responds, "Yes, which must be a nice vacation for his balls!" Paulette thanks Elle, smiling for the first time in the movie, and Elle realizes that a good lawyer can help those who need it most. At Christmas Elle and Paulette toast soda cans at the nail salon as their doggies and new besties Bruiser and Rufus join in the holiday fun.

The next semester Elle is indeed crushing it at Harvard Law, befriending recent alum Emmett (Luke Wilson) and even scoring a top internship with Professor Callahan (Victor Garber), whose firm is defending accused murderer, fitness guru, and Delta Nu alum Brooke Taylor-Windham (Ali Larter). Though Paulette now has her dog baby back, she *still* can't muster up the courage to chat with the UPS guy. All she can say is "Fine!" when he asks her how she's doing, or sometimes she says, "Okay!" That's progress, right?

*Unacceptable*, Elle decrees! Paulette has all the equipment, Elle says; she just needs to read the manual. While Bruiser and Rufus hang out, Elle instructs Paulette in the fine art of the "bend and snap"—an eye-catching move guaranteed to pull the attention and admiration of any crush. Though Paulette doesn't catch on right away, the whole salon gets into it to the tune of "Shake Your Moneymaker," and a hairstylist chimes in, "Oh my god, the bend and snap! Works every time!"

Brooke's murder trial kicks off, so Elle's busy at the courthouse, but meanwhile, Paulette applies makeup at the salon in anticipation of an extra-special delivery wearing snug brown shorts. Enter the UPS guy, who's visibly nervous—could he like Paulette back? "I've got a big one for you!" he blurts out, gesturing to the package she ordered. "Can you sign?"

Grinning widely, Paulette grabs a pen . . . and oh *no*, she drops it! The "bend and snap" moment has arrived! Paulette absolutely nails the bend—ten out of ten, gold medal, no notes. The snap, however . . . that's another story. The sexy UPS guy also turns out to be polite and kind, so while he bends down to grab the dropped pen, Paulette pops him in the face, breaking her crush's nose! "My snap was all over the place," Paulette moans to Elle over the phone.

Thankfully, UPS guy is undeterred, and his love is real. The next time we see Paulette is at the courthouse, as she attends Brooke's trial to support Elle, who's now Brooke's lawyer instead of creeper Callahan. Paulette has experienced a *glow-up*: instead of sad denim overalls, she's clad in a form-fitting purple dress and has the cutest accessory on her arm. No, it's not a purse—it's the UPS guy! He clearly adores her, despite the bandage on his nose (hey, love hurts sometimes).

Eventually, Elle's *Cosmo* girl knowledge of the simple and finite rules of hair care leads to an impromptu confession from Brooke's bitter stepdaughter, Chutney (Linda Cardellini), and Brooke is free. Flash forward to three years later, when Elle has a law degree, a prestigious job offer, and the privilege of being her graduating class's speaker. Paulette and the UPS guy—now married and expecting a daughter to be named Elle—look on proudly in the audience.

Though the newly named Paulette Parcelle doesn't have as much of a presence in *Legally Blonde 2: Red, White & Blonde*, she's still happily wedded to the UPS guy and a part of her bestie Elle's life. "You look like the Fourth of July!" Paulette exclaims upon seeing Elle's patriotic outfit in what is perhaps the sequel's most iconic bit of dialogue. "It makes me want a hot dog real bad."

## Why We Heart Paulette

Paulette is truly the best friend a blonde law student could have. She's also an excellent listener, whereas another manicurist might have mistaken bubbly Elle for a dim bulb—a common issue Elle faces throughout the movie—or written off her problems as silly nonissues for rich people. But if Paulette knows anything, it's heartbreak: though her relationship is very different from Elle's, she can still relate. From the moment they first meet, Paulette's kindness may be the only thing that keeps poor Elle from flying back to California instead of giving Harvard a real shot.

Paulette Bonafonté is one of Jennifer's most relatable characters. Who among us hasn't considered themselves unworthy after a brutal breakup? But we can all follow Paulette's example: make new friends who will always support us, stand up to bullies, and find love (both platonic and romantic) where we least expect it.

As Paulette, Jennifer combines pure silliness and unfiltered empathy—not an easy feat for any actor. With every sympathetic roll of her eyes, big nervous smile in the face of her crush, or game attempt at the bend and snap, Jennifer makes her way into every moviegoer's heart and establishes Paulette Bonafonté as a comedic sidekick for the ages. Elle Woods couldn't ask for a better friend. And of course, Jennifer's hair color fits right in—after all, blondes *do* have more fun!

## FUN BONUS FACTS

✱ IRL: Jennifer struggled to master the film's iconic "bend and snap." "Toni [Basil, the film's choreographer] was incredibly frustrated with my ability to handle the choreography," she told the *New York Times*. "Reese learned to 'bend and snap' in about 10 minutes and I was the antithesis of that." However, Basil was happy with Jennifer's performance: "Jennifer changed it around. She pushed up her [breasts] instead of snapping, because that's what Jennifer does, because that was right for the character."

✴ And of course, the bend and snap has now become a phenomenon. Jennifer said, "I could be on an airplane, seatbelted in, and they want me to get up and do it for them. Sometimes the requests are way more than you want to do during turbulence."

✴ Paulette's infatuation with the UPS guy didn't require much acting! "I had a crush on [Bruce Thomas, who played] my UPS man," Jennifer confessed to the *New York Times*. "I didn't have to act or get excited when he walked in—it was all true to life."

✴ Not only did Jennifer Coolidge reprise her role of Paulette in *Legally Blonde 2: Red, White & Blonde* (and according to interviews, she is open to appearing in *Legally Blonde 3*—Reese Witherspoon, take note!), but she also reprised the role in Ariana Grande's 2018 video for her hit single "Thank U, Next"! Jennifer told the *LA Times* podcast that she loved working with Ariana and was impressed by the song's take on relationships: if someone's not working for you, don't be afraid to move on. We think Paulette would heartily agree—she reclaimed her dog from her terrible ex, Dewey, and found love with someone who was worthy of her awesomeness.

# Amber Cole

## *A Mighty Wind* (2003)

Voluminous dark curly hair, tight black-and-white clothing with plenty of flashy jewelry, an accent of indeterminate origin, and a penchant for public relations—that's Amber Cole in a nutshell! Together, she and business partner Wally Fenton (Larry Miller) are tasked with publicizing a historic event. Well, historic to a niche community, anyway.

"Ode to Irving" is a one-night-only concert in memory of the recently deceased Irving Steinbloom, who represented the stars of the 1960s folk music scene, to be held at New York City's historic Town Hall. The show will be broadcast live, thanks to Swedish American folk groupie, dulcimer player, and one-hit wonder (with "How's It Hanging, Grandma?") Lars Olfen (Ed Begley Jr.), who now works in New York public television and loves nothing more than a good camera shot. Irving's neurotic son, Jonathan (Bob Balaban), is determined to make this the best night ever, roping in his estranged siblings (Don Lake and Deborah Theaker) to sit in the front row.

The concert consists of Irving's three favorite folk acts: The Folksmen, The Main Street Singers, and Mitch & Mickey, who made waves with their hit, "A Kiss at the End of the Rainbow." While The Folksmen are still friends and The Main Street Singers are actively performing as their second-generation iteration, The New Main Street Singers, Mitch & Mickey are a bit more complex: once real-life lovers, they had a tumultuous breakup back in the day. Mickey (Catherine O'Hara) is now happily married to bladder-device salesman and model-train enthusiast Leonard Crabbe (Jim Piddock), and Mitch (Eugene Levy) is . . . Well, no one really knows what Mitch is up to these days. Will The Folksmen and The New Main Street Singers butt heads when they perform the same tune? Will Mitch get it together enough to sing with Mickey again? And what of the real kiss that always accompanied their smash hit?

Backstage drama is of no concern to either Wally, who openly states his distaste for folk music, or Amber, who agrees with this sentiment with a hearty "Ohhhh, me too!" Once they've ensured that Town Hall tickets are sold and have had New York's deputy mayor declare "Folk Music Day in the Big Apple" to a sparse crowd, they've done their jobs. Time to raise a glass of white wine at the preshow soirée.

## *Why We Heart Amber*

In a cast of oddball and vibrant characters—type-A venue managers, eye-rolling family members, and performers who worship colors— Amber Cole holds her own. Though we only see her in a few scenes, she makes a strong impression, never letting anyone see her sweat and always smiling, flashing her brilliant white teeth. And teeth aren't the only asset Amber Cole proudly displays! As the saying goes, if you've got 'em, flaunt 'em, right?

Amber is also game for a good time. During the preshow party she makes conversation with Leonard Crabbe, expressing gratitude for the advent of model trains as he not so subtly checks out her heaving bosom. And of course, the concert is a rousing success and receives a standing ovation. Although we don't see Amber there, we know she did her part to put enthusiastic butts in the seats.

*A Mighty Wind* has a considerably different tone from *Best in Show*, Jennifer's first film with director Christopher Guest. Although both are mockumentaries, *Best in Show* has more biting satire, while *A Mighty Wind* leans hard into nostalgia and sentiment. But as Amber Cole—in all her tackily attired, ridiculously accented, cleavage-baring glory— Jennifer brings much-needed comic relief and keeps the story from getting too maudlin. For example, when Jonathan asks everyone to hum as a tribute to his father, Amber goes all the way, humming with her mouth wide open. In a film centered on music and emotion, Jennifer's flamboyant silliness is a breath of fresh air.

## FUN BONUS FACT

✳ Jennifer was good friends with comedic actor Fred Willard— they both appear in three Christopher Guest films, *Best in Show* (2000), *A Mighty Wind*, and *For Your Consideration* (2006), as well as the *American Pie* sequel *American Wedding* (2003), *Date Movie* (2006), and *Epic Movie* (2007). Willard passed away in 2020.

# Fiona Montgomery

## *A Cinderella Story* (2004)

### NOTABLE QUOTABLES

*"Oh, it's the Botox. I can't show emotion for
another hour and a half."*

-----------

*"You're not very pretty, and you're not very bright.
I'm so glad we had that talk."*

-----------

*"If you were part of my circus, I'd have you wiping
the elephant butts with a Wet One."*

When it comes to evil stepparents, Fiona Montgomery is the *mother* of
them all!

Fiona seems harmless when she first meets Hal Montgomery and
his sweet young daughter, Sam. She's tripping on a stairstep, adjusting
her glasses, and playing with her dull brown hair. Several years after the
wedding, however, it's a whole new story. After Hal passes away when
the Northridge Earthquake hits the family's San Fernando Valley home,
Fiona relegates teenaged Sam (Hilary Duff) to the house's attic and
forces her to work long hours at Hal's beloved diner while Fiona ter-
rorizes the adult employees, including Sam's favorite waitress and fairy
godmother, Rhonda (Regina King).

A now-bottle-blonde Fiona dives headfirst (and, um, boob first—thank you, surgeons of San Diego) into plastic surgery, even when she can't move her face from all the Botox. She gives Hal's Diner a terrifyingly pastel makeover and favors her tackily attired twin teenaged daughters, Brianna (Madeline Zima) and Gabriella (Andrea Avery), encouraging them to practice their synchronized swimming while making poor Sam wait on her hand and foot. And when Sam asks to leave work early to go to a special school dance, where she'll finally meet the secret admirer who she's been corresponding with over Instant Messenger, Fiona expressly forbids it without even leaving her favorite backyard tanning bed—which is pink, of course.

Sam sneaks out of work and makes it to the dance in a gorgeous, borrowed dress. However, she must make it back to the diner by midnight, when Fiona comes in to watch the staff like a bottle-blonde hawk. And because it's a masked ball, Sam leaves her secret admirer, popular and sensitive football player Austin (Chad Michael Murray), without revealing her identity. Things get even more complicated when Fiona's daughters find out Sam's been corresponding with Austin—and of course, Fiona can't let this go. The vengeful Fiona hides Sam's acceptance letter from Princeton and presents her with a fake rejection letter instead, crushing her stepdaughter's academic dreams and pretending to be sympathetic.

After Brianna and Gabriella falsely accuse Sam of vandalizing Hal's Diner, Sam says enough is enough: "You know what, Fiona? You can mess with your hair and your nose and your face, and can even mess with my dad's diner, but you're through messing with me!" She quits the diner, moves in with kind waitress Rhonda (who, along with the rest of

the diner staff, quits in solidarity with Sam), reconnects with Austin, and accepts her acceptance to Princeton. Sam went through a lot, and she learns the importance of making her own happy ending.

As for Fiona? She doesn't get away with her awful treatment of Sam over the years. Sam finds out that *she* owns Hal's Diner, not Fiona, and Fiona's relentless insistence that her teen stepdaughter work as much as possible actually violates child labor laws. And because Sam owns the house and cars as well, Sam sells Fiona and her stepsisters' vehicles to pay for Princeton.

Instead of going to jail, Fiona makes a deal with the district attorney: working long hours at Hal's Diner alongside her daughters! Guess you better learn to scrub floors, Fiona, because eventually, *all* wicked stepmothers get exactly what they deserve—and it's *not* a happily ever after.

## *Why We Heart Fiona*

At first one may think: *An evil stepmother? What exactly is there to heart?*

Well, she's not a regular evil stepmom; she's a *hilarious* evil stepmom—all because of Jennifer Coolidge's fabulous sense of fun, ability to rock heinous early-aughts fashion, and straight-up mastery of every script she takes on. Thanks to Jennifer's extraordinary comic timing, there's a whole lot to heart about Fiona. The best kind of villain is a funny one, and Fiona's up there with the best—or *worst*—of them.

Just like the diner she presides over, this wicked stepmama's signature color is pink. From her nails to her lips to her tanning bed, Fiona Montgomery is an evil pink queen whose twisted fashion and beauty sense you can't help but admire, even when she's yelling at Sam to clean the swimming pool or blatantly ignoring the California drought in favor of keeping her lawn bright green: "Droughts are for poor people. You think J.Lo has a brown lawn? People who use extra water have extra class!"

Even at her meanest, there's no denying Fiona's hilariously terrible fashion sense, which would easily rise to the top of any worst-dressed list! Pink vinyl and marabou are the stars of the tacky show, along with a lot of low-cut necklines to show off Fiona's fake *assets* (procured in San Diego, thank you very much). Fiona sits by the pool, reading about the latest trendy diet (salmon, by the way) in a giant pair of sunglasses and an impractical lace outfit—all the better to order Sam around in. If it's the worst of the early aughts, Fiona's wearing it—yet somehow Jennifer Coolidge makes it all look fab.

While she's bullying Sam, Fiona never fails to entertain the audience—driving recklessly because she can't feel her increasingly plasticized face, nomming on the cookies (Jennifer improvised the iconic line, "Mmm, they're so moist") that are *supposed* to be for comforting her stepdaughter over her "rejection" from Princeton ("Well, just look at the bright side: you have a job at the diner for the rest of your life!"), and telling Sam, "You're not very pretty and you're not very bright," when in fact, *Fiona* looks like a fool in her tiny red tanning goggles.

Jennifer ensures that Fiona is not a scary villain but a comic one—a woman the audience absolutely loves to hate while they crack up at every mean thing she says to her stepdaughter and every frozen facial expression or pink-tinged pratfall. The laughs never stop and, thanks to Jennifer's fabulous delivery, watching this evil stepmother get her comeuppance is nothing short of joyful.

## FUN BONUS FACTS

✳ Jennifer is allergic to glue, so Fiona's fake fingernails had to be attached with tape.

✳ Samantha, Fiona, and the stepsisters each have a distinctive color palette in the film. Sam primarily wears blue, the stepsisters red and green, and Fiona is mostly in pink. This directly corresponds to the same characters in the 1950 Disney animated film *Cinderella*.

✳ Both Jennifer and costar Regina King appeared in *Legally Blonde 2: Red, White & Blonde*.

# Aunt Fanny

## *Robots* (2005)

Aunt Fanny is as generous as her red (sometimes pink) and white posterior. With dark blue eyes and a curvy, colorful figure, this automaton resembles a snail, but she is so much more. As a character in the movie states, Aunt Fanny has her name because they can't call her Aunt Booty. She's a creatively attired, proud mother figure to the Rusties—a ragtag group of outdated, outmoded robots—and she lets them stay in her boardinghouse outside of Rivet Town while treating them as her own family. In Aunt Fanny's opinion, everyone needs love and support.

Aunt Fanny is known for her—well, there's no other way to say it— *talent* for passing gas. When the Rusties hold a farting contest, they are no match for Aunt Fanny's big, beautiful booty. Sure, she accidentally kills a streetlamp in her quest for the gold, but it's just a testament to all that talent, which can be as much of a burden as it is a gift.

"Fighting never solves anything!" Aunt Fanny proclaims (another great life lesson from Ms. New Booty herself). Still, when the going gets tough, Aunt Fanny and her gas get going! In the movie's climactic fight scene, Aunt Fanny shows up to help defeat the evil Madame Gasket and her army of henchmen—using nothing but her powerful rear end. And when it's all over, Aunt Fanny accepts a dance from—and makes a love connection with—Bigweld (Mel Brooks), the head of a company devoted to making the metal folks' lives better.

## Why We Heart Aunt Fanny

For far too long, there has been an extreme double standard when it comes to, um, passing gas. When men (or male-identified members of any species) do it, it's hilarious, but when their female counterparts fart, it's considered gross and unladylike. Aunt Fanny is here to kick that ridiculousness squarely in the metal, well, *fanny*!

Not only is Aunt Fanny a standout character, she represents another opportunity for Jennifer to show off her unique voice, her extraordinary line readings, and her exuberant, take-no-prisoners personality. A hallmark of a Jennifer Coolidge character is someone who's unapologetically herself, and Aunt Fanny is no different. When you've got that much gorgeous, red-and-white, studded junk in the trunk, why not show the world exactly what said junk is capable of? Combined with Jennifer's fantastic distinctive voice-over, behold: a farting star is born. We love you forever, Jennifer and Aunt Fanny! Never stop toot-toot-tooting away!

## FUN BONUS FACTS

✳ In the UK, "fanny" is a euphemism for a private part found on folks assigned female at birth. Definitely not a word that children are supposed to go around saying! Therefore, Jennifer's *Robots* character is called "Aunt Fan" in the UK version of the film and its corresponding game. (Funnily enough, "Aunt Fan" was the character's original name, until the studio changed it.)

✳ *Robots* wasn't the last anyone heard of Aunt Fanny and her farts. Jennifer went on to voice the character in the *Robots* video game as well as the short spin-off film *Aunt Fanny's Tour of Booty* (2005).

✳ Though Jennifer had done voice work on television, Aunt Fanny was her first voice acting role in a theatrical film (and that of her costars Jim Broadbent, Paul Giamatti, and Harland Williams), but it certainly wasn't her last. Since then Jennifer has had many voice roles in films and television shows, including *Dr. Doolittle: Tail to the Chief* (2008), *LEGO Hero Factory: Rise of the Rookies* (2010), and the *Napoleon Dynamite* animated series (2012).

# Judith Purvis

## *Gentlemen Broncos* (2009)

In the small Utah mountain town of Saltair, in a round white house lives an imaginative homeschooled teenager named Benjamin Purvis (Michael Angarano) and his scrappy single mom, Judith. They were left behind by the Purvis patriarch, a brave, bearded explorer. Benjy and Judith don't have much money, but they have their dreams.

Mother and son are creators: Benjy's passion is writing his own science fiction and fantasy stories, the most recent being *Yeast Lords*, about a brave, bearded explorer on a quest with a unique pair of siblings, a killer kittycat, and copious flatulence. Judith can do amazing things with a popcorn ball and sells modest nightgowns for a living, but she fantasizes about making her *own* nightgowns and other garments for women.

Sketches for her debut line, Decent Beginnings, are lovingly preserved in a padded, eyelet-fabric-covered album. In the meantime, she scrimps and saves to send Benjy to Cletus Fest, an out-of-town writing conference for teens, where he can meet his hero, author Dr. Ronald

Chevalier. She even coughs up forty bucks for Benjy to have food, even though she thought four would be enough.

When Benjy returns, Judith has a surprise for him. She's noticed that he doesn't really have friends, so through church she procured him a Guardian Angel—a Big Brother–type figure who will hang out with Benjy and enrich his fragile young mind. Dusty (Mike White) has majestic, long blond curly hair and a mustache to match. Little does Judith know, however, that Dusty has poison darts hidden in his boat of a car—and when one accidentally hits Judith in the chesticle area, her water bra saves the day.

Judith doesn't give up on her son, even when everyone around Benjy lets him down, including a pair of conniving teenaged filmmakers who use a bad check to option *Yeast Lords* for a low-budget movie, with Dusty starring as the hero, Bronco. She's excited for the film's local premiere and even sews Benjy a festive shirt, complete with giant white rickrack piping. And of course, Judith whips up her own dress to match.

Though the local Saltair film premiere is a bust—and what's worse, Benjy's hero, Dr. Ronald Chevalier, plagiarizes *Yeast Lords* for himself—Benjy realizes how much Judith loves him, and he immediately returns the favor. When evil, rich Don Carlos (John Baker) lures her to his mansion under the guise of giving Judith's clothing line the big break it deserves—when he *really* wants to get under her modest, long skirt—Benjy, who's come along for the ride, saves his mother from harm, using Dusty's special poison darts.

Benjy is dismayed to land in jail, on his birthday to boot, but Judith has a surprise in store. Spoiler alert: it's not the miniature car she's crafted for him out of popcorn, though that *is* pretty sweet. The present, as Benjy discovers, will save his writing for good.

## *Why We Heart Judith*

Relentlessly positive and optimistic, Judith never lets a lack of money or resources get her down, except when she's dressed in her own home-made clothes, watching herself cry. She's an exceptionally loving mom to Benjy—she even brings him presents when he lands in jail on his birthday. Judith believes in them both and their ability to succeed and make art.

And in the end, Judith saves the day with one of these presents: since he was seven years old, she's registered every one of Benjy's sto-ries with the Writers' League, proving that the story in question is his own and not Dr. Ronald Chevalier's. Benjy becomes a published author and surprises Judith with a fashion show of her very own designs, with Dusty as one of the models. And the way Judith eyes Dusty in the film's final moments tells us there may be a romance happening very soon . . .

*Gentlemen Broncos* is chock-full of quirky characters and settings, and as Judith Purvis, Jennifer dives in headfirst, resulting in the film's most memorable performance. Jennifer's unique delivery and unmis-takable grin give Judith that extra something special. Thanks to Jen, the audience sees Judith as a very devoted mother with a distinct sense of style: modest and church-friendly while also colorful and happy. Throughout the movie Jennifer looks fantastic in Judith's getups of embroidered flowers, pretty pastels, and the occasional shiny fab-ric. Even better than the clothes are how Jennifer embodies Judith's generosity with her loved ones through dialogue and loving looks to her little boy. Moms are everyday superheroes, and thanks to Jennifer's happy and genuine portrayal, Judith is the most powerful of them all.

## FUN BONUS FACTS

✳ Judith's sunny nature may have come from Jennifer herself: Jennifer loved working on this movie. She told *Deadline* in 2022 that it was the most fun she'd ever had on set. And with her massive talent and visible joy, Jennifer made amazing connections. *Gentlemen Broncos* was directed by Jared Hess and written by Jared and Jerusha Hess, the dream team behind the early-aughts cult classic *Napoleon Dynamite*. She would go on to provide a voice in *Napoleon Dynamite: The Animated Series*, and a decade after *Gentlemen Broncos* Jennifer would work with Jerusha Hess again on the rom-com *Austenland*.

✳ Jen met writer/director/actor Mike White while working on *Gentlemen Broncos*, and after sharing several scenes in the film, the two became good friends. Eventually Jennifer and Mike, who share a deep love of animals, would go on vacation together on an African safari. The fun they had together, coupled with Jennifer's memorable remarks on the trip, inspired Mike to write Tanya on *The White Lotus* especially for her to play.

# Miss Elizabeth Charming

*Austenland* (2013)

Who cares if she's never read *Pride and Prejudice*? Who cares if she doesn't know what *Pride and Prejudice* is? Miss Elizabeth Charming—the moniker she specifically requested—has paid for the platinum package at

Austenland, an immersive experience at a large rural English estate where women can enjoy old-fashioned romance, a grand ball, and a happy ending. "I'm gonna look great in those wench gowns," Miss Charming enthuses before even setting foot in Austenland. "I hope they give me a cape too!"

From the second she appears at the London airport in a hot pink frock and matching fascinator with plenty of feathers, it's clear that Miss Charming is the perfect foil for Jane, aka Miss Erstwhile (Keri Russell), a serious Austen fangirl who, despite spending her life's savings on Austenland, *cannot* afford the platinum package. While Miss Erstwhile is relegated to the servants' quarters, an unflattering hairstyle, and a dull-brown excuse for a gown, Miss Charming is living her best life.

Miss Elizabeth Charming spends her time in Austenland decked out in various shades of pink and lavender—with a tightly laced corset underneath for maximum cleavage—complete with matching hair flowers, bonnets, very tall headpieces, and, of course, feathers. At one point she even sports a taxidermized bird in her fabulous blonde coif. "Look how skinny I look with my hand behind my back!" she exclaims while admiring herself in a full-length mirror.

Miss Charming is *all in* on the various Austenland activities, making kissy faces at groundskeeper/driver Martin (Bret McKenzie) and flirting up a storm—including initiating a saucy game of footsie at the very first dinner—with various suitors (paid actors) on the estate. "RIGHT-O!" she enthuses in her best attempt at a British accent. "I sure would like you to turn me upside down in the garden!"

Okay, she doesn't love *all* the activities designated for the ladies of Austenland. Horseback hunt? Yes! ("Can you believe it? Real horses and real guns!") Embroidery? Ick! Miss Charming can only come up with a tangled knot of thread—pink, of course. And when Lady Amelia Heartwright (Georgia King) sings off-key, Miss Charming not so subtly requests, "Please shut your hole." That's not the last time she puts Lady Heartwright in her place. While the ladies are fashioning their own headpieces, Miss Charming admonishes, "Don't copy *everything* I do!" It's all about the suitors for Miss Charming: "If the men don't come back from hunting soon, I'm gonna ask for a refund."

When a theatrical (live play/performance) is announced for the suitors and female participants, Miss Charming is all too happy to play Aphrodite, the goddess of love and (at least she likes to think) the play's central character. Onstage Miss Charming–as–Aphrodite emerges from a life-size shell, rocking a long red wig, waving a wand with a giant pearl on top, and mispronouncing the word "largesse." "I shall make everything all right-y because I am the beautiful Aphrodite!" she proclaims, inexpertly shooting a bow and arrow toward the actors playing the star-crossed lovers.

"I was aiming for your cans, because they're such a small target," she informs Amelia before pulling out one of the lady's cutlets and then gouging out her eye in a most unladylike tussle. Miss Charming then sings and shimmies until the curtain comes down. A command performance indeed.

At Austenland's final ball Miss Charming makes her big move on the actor playing Colonel Andrews (James Callis). When he calls her his Venus de Milo, she leans in for a passionate kiss. How was Miss Charming to know she was behaving inappropriately? As Miss Erstwhile is

packing to leave, she gently informs Miss Charming that Colonel Andrews might not return her feelings (he *is* a paid actor, after all). Miss Charming is tremendously relieved to hear this: "I was so worried you were going to say he was gay."

At the end, the wealthy Miss Charming has bought Austenland from the evil Wattlesbrooks (Jane Seymour and Rupert Vansittart) and converted it into a more fun place, with pink and yellow décor, cotton candy, swan boats, and even a sexy striptease from Captain East (Ricky Whittle). She exclaims while surrounded by footmen, "This is truly my fantasy!"

Miss Charming is last seen hoofing it to Nelly's "Hot in Herre" over the closing credits, wearing a lavender gown and wielding a large fan.

## *Why We Heart Miss Charming*

Miss Elizabeth Charming is the original good-time gal. She brings a sense of joy and fun to every situation, whether it's heckling a lady's singing voice to gamely dressing up as Aphrodite, to getting her groove on at the final ball. From the moment we meet her, we know that Miss Elizabeth Charming is the perfect foil to the intense Jane/Miss Erstwhile, as well as the best person to show her not to take Austenland— and life—too seriously.

Miss Charming is a most excellent friend to Miss Erstwhile. She consoles Miss Erstwhile after the latter has a disastrous first dinner with the male suitors: "I know how it feels to be treated badly by stupid men—I do!" And when Jane/Miss Erstwhile decides to make her own happy ending here at Austenland, Miss Charming sneaks into Lady Heartwright's bedchambers and "borrows" fabulous gowns and hats for

Jane to make herself over. She even tries to teach Jane how to speak in a British accent: "Bloody Americans, grrr!"

Jane/Miss Erstwhile appreciates the gift that is Miss Charming. The more skilled at needlework of the two, Jane presents Miss Charming with a lovely cross-stitch of her face. "That's beautiful!" Miss Charming exclaims. "I think she's way prettier than me, don't you think?" After Miss Charming buys Austenland, Jane returns with her now-IRL suitor, Mr. Henry Nobley (JJ Feild).

*Austenland* was a return to form for Jennifer, who came up as an improviser—according to IMDb, she made up most of her hilarious dialogue. The film's producers said it was almost impossible to get her to memorize the script. Hey, you can't keep a funny lady down! With a constant run of sassy quips, phenomenal facial expressions, and incredible fashion moments, Jennifer proves she is up for anything as a comedic actor, and the film is all the better for it. Not to mention she brings every ounce of her theatrical training to the scene-stealing, bewigged mighty Aphrodite.

The movie is also a reunion of Jennifer and director Jerusha Hess, who cowrote the film *Gentlemen Broncos* with her husband, Jared Hess. Jennifer has spoken in interviews about how much she loved working with the Hesses on *Gentlemen Broncos* (which also featured Jennifer's future *White Lotus* collaborator, Mike White), and the party continues in *Austenland*. Here, Jennifer shows off her versatility: no longer the frumpy single mom of *Gentlemen Broncos*, she's a wealthy lady on the prowl who embraces everything, from riding horses to wearing bonnets to wildly flirting with open arms and white-gloved hands. Jennifer and Jerusha had a blast working on *Austenland*, and so, in turn, does *Austenland*'s audience watching the film.

**FUN BONUS FACT**

✳ *Flight of the Conchords* fans, look no further than Miss Coolidge's filmography. She's appeared in films with both Bret McKenzie (*Austenland*) and Jemaine Clement (*Gentlemen Broncos*). These films were the brainchild of married couple Jared and Jerusha Hess.

# Susan Thomas

## *Promising Young Woman* (2020)

---

### NOTABLE QUOTABLES

*"What kind of person forgets their thirtieth birthday?"*

------------

*"Now I'm confused. Are there different
parts of the body on a child?"*

---

Susan just wants her daughter to be okay. Ever since Cassandra (Carey Mulligan) dropped out of medical school without explanation and returned home to her parents, she spends her days working in a pastel-colored café, and Cassie's nights remain a mystery. The once-promising young woman even forgot her own birthday. Susan knows something's up, but what's a mother to do with an adult daughter who won't confide in her?

To Cassie's credit and Susan's satisfaction, the former *does* eat breakfast with her parents every morning before heading off to her minimum-wage job. When Susan and Cassie's father, Stanley (Clancy Brown), present Cassie with a big pink suitcase at breakfast on Cassie's birthday—which Cassie later remarks is "the fanciest get-the-fuck-out-of-our-house metaphor I've ever seen" to her manager and friend Gail (Laverne Cox)—Susan hits a wall.

"What kind of person forgets their thirtieth birthday?" she frantically asks her daughter, who responds that it's not a big deal. "Not a big deal? You just forgot your birthday! You don't want to have a party? You don't want to see your friends?" Susan's practically in tears: *What exactly is going on here? What's happened to Cassie?*

Susan doesn't get answers but *is* happy when Cassie heads out to lunch with former med school classmate Ryan Cooper (Bo Burnham) and is positively ecstatic when Cassie brings her now-boyfriend home for dinner. Susan prepares pasta—Stanley made the sauce, which Ryan praises—and wears a nice outfit and pearls, her brunette pageboy hairstyle smooth and impeccable. She even laughs at his jokes and asks, "What kind of doctoring do you do?" Later Cassie jokes to Ryan, "I think she likes you more than I do."

Of course, Susan is heartbroken when Cassie goes missing. "It's not like her to disappear like this," she tearfully tells the authorities. "You know, she was getting better. She was, really." When the police ask Susan and Stanley whether Cassie was dating anyone, Susan opens her mouth to speak. It's assumed she leads the authorities to Ryan, who knows exactly what happened—unbeknownst to Susan, Cassie spent her nights exacting revenge against the same type of men who harmed her best friend and med school classmate, Nina, and Cassie did not survive her most elaborate revenge scheme yet. Little does everyone know that Cassie gets the last laugh from beyond the grave, and hopefully Susan will receive the closure she deserves.

# Why We Heart Susan

At her core Susan is a good mom in a bad situation. She wants to be there for her daughter, even though she doesn't know the whole story of why Cassie is the way she is. And because Cassie is thirty years old now, she doesn't have to confide in her mom, no matter how much Susan wants her to. Cassie also doesn't have to tell Susan about her nights as an avenging angel, enacting revenge on men like the one who hurt Cassie's best friend.

*Promising Young Woman* is a departure for Jennifer as an actress, and a brilliant one at that. Though this is far from her first dramatic role—or at least a less-funny role, as the film could also be considered a dark comedy—Jen's more known for her comedic performances. Susan is a smaller part, but Jennifer shows a deep sense of character and empathy while also providing small moments of levity, a must in such an intense film.

Later, audiences would see this in *The White Lotus*'s Tanya McQuoid. Though Tanya has a completely different personality and fate, Jennifer's same ability to penetrate the depths behind the dialogue shines through, as it does in *Promising Young Woman*. Susan—and Jennifer—are a testament to the adage, "There are no small parts, only small actors."

## FUN BONUS FACTS

✳ At one point Cassandra's new boyfriend, Ryan (Bo Burnham), tells Cassie that her mom is sexy. Not only is that the truth, but it's also a reference to Jennifer's hot AF breakout turn as Stifler's Mom in *American Pie*.

✳ Two other actresses in the film, Connie Britton and Molly Shannon, also appear in season one of *The White Lotus*.

✳ *Promising Young Woman* is Jennifer's fifth movie to be nominated for at least one Academy Award® and the second to win—in this case, Best Original Screenplay.

✳ According to an interview with *Screen Rant* magazine, Jennifer was excited to work with writer and director Emerald Fennell after seeing Fennell's short film *Careful as You Go* and reading *Promising Young Woman*'s script, which Jennifer told the magazine "just didn't remind me of anything I had read."

✳ Filming the role of Susan only required Jennifer to be on set for a week, so she didn't see the entire film until it premiered in New York City. Jennifer was blown away by the finished product, saying, "I went in that theater, saw the movie, and I just couldn't get out of my chair when it ended."

# Aunt Sandy

## *Single All the Way* (2021)

---

### NOTABLE QUOTABLES

*"All the world's a stage, and most of us are desperately unrehearsed."*

- - - - - - - - - - -

*"The gays just know how to do stuff.
They're survivors. And for some reason, they're always
obsessed with me."*

- - - - - - - - - - -

*"Be right back. Or not. I've been making eyes with a very
handsome man, and now it's time to land a plane."*

---

Aunt Sandy is the unofficial *grande dame* of small-town New Hampshire, where she returned after a less-than-illustrious career in the New York theater (though she *did* understudy Audrey in an off-Broadway production of *Little Shop of Horrors*). Now Aunt Sandy directs the town's annual Christmas pageant and gives it her all, even when cast members—usually whatever nieces, nephews, and other kids and teens she can rope in—are reluctant to learn their lines.

Never mind the obstacles, Sandy is determined to make this year's production of *Jesus H. Christ!* (the exclamation point is intentional) a smash hit—as opposed to "a giant load of crap on a stick, and not in a good way," as she deems the play after an especially rough rehearsal.

Assisting with this year's pageant are Aunt Sandy's adult nephew, Peter (who was her very first Joseph when he was younger—that year the pageant was a "play within a play" that took place *backstage* at a Christmas pageant)—and Peter's best friend, Nick. They are both visiting from Los Angeles for the holidays, as Peter (Michael Urie) has just gotten dumped by his boyfriend, who turned out to be married, and is dodging his loving family's efforts to fix him up.

He's also in denial about his own feelings for Nick (Philemon Chambers) and is thinking he'd like to move back to New Hampshire, so the Christmas pageant is a perfect distraction. Plus, Peter's a social media manager and great with aesthetics—and bribing his nieces and nephews with Christmas cookies so they'll learn their lines. And Nick, a children's book author who works as a handyman on the side, is a whiz at building a life-size manger for the baby Jesus.

On Christmas Eve Aunt Sandy rouses the troops with her usual pep talk—which, as Peter alerts Nick, is, word for word, Madonna's preshow prayer from the *Truth or Dare* documentary—before making a stunning entrance onstage. Aunt Sandy narrates the story of Jesus, Mary, and Joseph while dressed as Glinda the Good Witch herself. After the play, which is a success just as she knew it would be, Aunt Sandy has a missed connection after assuming that personal trainer James (Luke Macfarlane) is interested in her—he's actually into her nephew, Peter. Undeterred, Aunt Sandy closes the movie with a spirited onstage dance at the local bar. Merry Christmas, one and all!

## *Why We Heart Aunt Sandy*

We heart a diva, and Aunt Sandy is the biggest that New England's ever seen. (At least in her own head.)

Aunt Sandy's sense of style is fabulous from head to toe. First, she sports a fiercely curled blonde bob, complemented by mile-long eyelashes—that probably aren't real, but honestly, who cares?—and giant gold star-shaped earrings, which she stole from the family Christmas tree, but honestly, who cares? Over the course of *Single All the Way*, she sports a tight leopard-print wiggle dress *and* a leopard-print coat on top (at this moment Nick, who's meeting Aunt Sandy for the first time, looks at Peter and says, "I love her!"), a green snake-print dress, and a dragonfly-print coat. Her outfits are perpetually topped off with the most magnificent of accessories: a burgundy fur wrap. It *is* winter, after all, and even divas must stay warm.

Although Aunt Sandy can be more of a *dictator* than a *director*—she tells her young cast, "I didn't want to mention punishment, but I can tell you I'm really scary!"—she's one thousand percent committed to making *Jesus H. Christ!* the best Christmas pageant ever. Inspired by Whitney Houston's cover of "Joy to the World"—because, as Aunt Sandy gushes to her family, "It has everything: the king, the savior, the glory, and the born!"—the pageant earns rave reviews from the townspeople, prompting Aunt Sandy to consider the grandest move of all: a national tour.

Did we mention Aunt Sandy is also a fierce ally? When she hears Peter is going out on a date, she enthusiastically asks him, "Like from Grindr?" Stereotypical small-town mentality begone.

It's not just the gays: We're *all* obsessed with Jennifer Coolidge, and seeing her in a Christmas movie is the best gift of all. *Single All the Way's* script is sharp and funny, but TBH, Jennifer could have improvised her entire role, as she's done multiple times for Christopher Guest, and Aunt Sandy would have been just as delightful and memorable. It's a rare actress who can make leopard print look festive; who can speak in italics, capital letters, and an old-movie accent that would make Bette Davis proud (or jealous); who can pull off a Glinda the Good Witch gown; and who can end the entire movie lasciviously backup dancing for a well-known comic musician. Jen truly does it *all* in this film. Even when she yells at children, we want more.

Most of all, our beloved J. Cool now has a spot in the Christmas movie canon—a new holiday tradition for us all to enjoy. Jennifer is so perfectly cast in this movie, it's almost unreal. Jennifer Coolidge bless us, every one.

# Carol Fowler

## *Shotgun Wedding* (2022)

---

### NOTABLE QUOTABLES

*"I've been looking forward to this moment ever since baby Tommy was cut out of my abdomen."*

------------

*"When I'm in formalwear, I like to pee standing up. How about you?"*

------------

*"I'm a mother. I can worry about a lot of things at the same time, like Larry's mole."*

---

Carol Fowler is *so excited* to be here—a destination wedding at the Mahal Island Resort in the Philippines. Carol has never left the country or been to an island, unless you count Mackinac Island in Carol's home state of Michigan, which Carol does *not*. The groom is Carol's son, Tom (Josh Duhamel), a baseball player recently cut from the minor leagues at forty years old (ouch), who is marrying power lawyer Darcy Rivera (Jennifer Lopez). Couldn't you just die? Hopefully, no one will this weekend.

While everyone else at the rehearsal dinner sports tasteful pastels and florals, Carol bursts in wearing bold zebra stripes while trilling, "I'm Gonna Wash That Man Right Outta My Hair." (She tried to start a *South Pacific* sing-along on the boat ride over, much to the chagrin of Darcy's mother, Renata [Sonia Braga], who is the height of taste and class.) Carol's beloved husband and Tom's father, Larry (Steve Coulter), is enthusiastically capturing the festivities on an old-school video camera, which hopefully won't run out of batteries. While Darcy didn't want a wedding at all, let alone one so elaborate—her divorced, still-feuding parents may have something to do with that—Tom wants to emulate his mom and dad's own loving marriage, hence the fancy nuptials.

Speaking of love, Carol proudly presents Darcy with a special gift: a set of rusty wedding-cake knives, wrapped in scratchy white tulle for the occasion. Everyone in the Fowler family has used these very knives, Carol enthuses to a less-than-thrilled Darcy. In fact, these knives bring good luck, Carol says, "Except for Uncle Greg, who got decapitated on a forklift."

Carol is supportive during the requisite rehearsal dinner speeches, laughing at her boy's bumbling puns while Larry falls asleep holding the video camera. When Tom and Darcy are getting ready for bed, Carol comes in with extras for the welcome bags and astutely informs her son, "Tommy, she's not wearing any pants," before admiring her soon-to-be daughter-in-law's exquisite posterior. Unfortunately for the lovers, Carol decrees that they cannot spend the night together. Unlike the family wedding-cake knives, this *is* bad luck. After all, Carol recalls, Tom's cousin Jenna *did* bed down the night before her wedding, only to get Lyme disease, and now she can't wear sandals.

The next morning it's wedding-prep time. Carol is excited once again because Darcy is wearing Carol's own wedding dress: a vision in off-white, with balloon sleeves and a neckline that can only be described as *low*. "I Scotchgarded the dress," Carol warns the bride, "so try not to inhale any chemicals." Carol also arranges Darcy's tresses in a majestic updo with a generous dose of hairspray (Darcy later remarks to Tom, "Now birds are gonna lay eggs in it"). Carol is clad in a pastel-green, flowered, tight dress—with a matching hat, of course.

All the beautiful Michigan-made frocks in the world, however, cannot cancel out Carol's mounting sense of dread. "I have a bad feeling about this," she remarks to her husband as the guests assemble. Meanwhile, Tom and Darcy are nowhere to be found—unbeknownst to everyone, they're alone again and on the verge of breaking it off for good. Just then, Carol sees a rapidly approaching ship and screams because she sees . . .

Pirates!

These aren't funny *Peter Pan*–type pirates. These are masked thieves with machine guns, who force the terrified guests into the resort's infinity pool while also capturing Tom and Darcy in their room, mid-argument. Why are they here? Turns out, Darcy's father, Robert (Cheech Marin), has a multimillion-dollar fortune—but not for long, if the pirates have anything to say about it. The pirates may not have known which hostage was Robert, but a helpful Carol alerts the bad guys to his presence. Robert refuses to surrender the funds until he knows his daughter is safe and unharmed, so the scared hostages remain in the infinity pool.

Carol, though still afraid, is *not* going to take this lying down. "Come out, Mr. Pirate Man!" she calls from her place in the pool. "My name is Carol Elaine Fowler, and I deserve to live!" Carol goes on to list her impressive credentials—wife, mother of two, and Milford, Michigan's top Realtor in 1998 *and* 2007, thank you very much. She then shares her big

dream—going to Ireland—as well as an embarrassing fact: she is a late bloomer whose teeth didn't come in until she was fourteen years old.

Carol alerts the pirates and her fellow hostages that she's just doing what she saw on *Good Morning America*: humanizing herself so she'll be allowed to live. Always the trendsetter, Carol inspires other hostages to introduce themselves as well. A man of few words, her spouse shares, "I'm Larry Fowler. Thank you."

While Carol and the rest of the guests are stuck in the pool, Darcy and Tom must evade their own kidnappers *and* work on their relationship—all while dressed for a ceremony that may or may not still happen. Thanks to a stealth move on Darcy's part—setting a pirate's head on fire with a lit cigarette—the still-feuding couple is now free, albeit tied together and making their way through the dense jungle. Once they're back at the resort, Darcy attempts to cut off their zip ties with a very special weapon—a Fowler family cake knife. It doesn't work, but it's the thought that counts.

Eventually Tom finds himself at the pool with the other hostages while Darcy hides, and the truth comes out: Darcy's smoking-hot but vindictive ex, Sean (Lenny Kravitz), was behind the pirating scheme and is the reason the bad guys are holding out for the multimillion-dollar bounty rather than just looting and leaving, as pirates typically do. Unfortunately, Sean has escaped along with Robert's yoga teacher girlfriend, Harriet (D'Arcy Carden), who was the dastardly Sean's accomplice.

Darcy arrives at the scene and has nabbed a shotgun of her own. She tearfully confesses to Tom that she didn't want a big wedding, but she also doesn't want to lose him, while a still-wet Carol remarks, "This is so much better than *South Pacific!*" Darcy worries that she and Tom can never live up to the Fowlers' perfect marriage, and another truth comes out.

Larry and Carol reveal that their relationship, while filled with love, has been anything but easy. Back in the day Larry slept with Carol's sister, Tom's aunt Marie, and in turn, Carol started doing what she terms "weird sex stuff" with a neighbor, Jim Roberts. Larry recalls that Carol's affair went on for a couple of months, at least, and Carol says, "Because our bodies just fit." In the end, Aunt Marie had a sex addiction, and Jim Roberts wasn't endgame for Carol, so the Fowlers lived happily ever after. And they hope Darcy and Tom can too.

Newly heartened, Darcy and Tom decide to tie the knot after all, with unexpected pirate guests. Carol is game, even starting a sing-along of the late-nineties classic "I'll Be" as Darcy makes her way down the makeshift aisle. What Carol *doesn't* know is that Darcy and Tom have a plan: to bum-rush the pirates while Darcy grabs a grenade. Darcy orders the pirates to drop their guns, but one of them runs away and starts shooting.

He's gonna regret that, because IT'S CAROL TIME. Fed up with all the shenanigans, the mother of the groom grabs a discarded rifle, declares, "Nobody fucks with my family!" and starts shooting. Truly a boss move.

Per Darcy's request, Carol—gun still in hand—goes to protect the rest of the scattered wedding party. Before she leaves, Darcy shows Carol the family cake knife that she has been carrying with her all along. She thanks Carol with a vehement: "I fucking love this cake knife!"

Finally, the authorities arrive and the chaos ends. Darcy and Tom get married for real, to the delight of their families and friends, especially Carol. At the reception everyone sings and dances to the eighties bop "Walk Like an Egyptian"—as Larry films enthusiastically, of course.

## *Why We Heart Carol*

Carol. Contains. Multitudes. Who else can expertly wield a machine gun in a mint-green gown? She's devoted to her son and family, which now includes her daughter-in-law, Darcy. Carol will do anything for her people, whether it's traveling to a remote island in the Philippines for the ultimate destination wedding, humanizing herself to a crew of deadly masked men, or using a weapon to protect them all—without messing up her hair.

Carol's unashamed of her libido—hey, Jim Roberts came into her life for a reason—but is also realistic, knowing that great times in bed don't necessarily equal a happily ever after. She and Frank chose one another and continue to do so as a united front for their two kids. And what do you know: those cake knives really were good luck. There's no doubt that Carol will regale her friends and real estate colleagues with wild tales of the shotgun wedding once she returns to Michigan. And hopefully, she'll wear that magnificent frock again.

*Shotgun Wedding* is a wild ride from beginning to end, and *everyone* on that island has feelings, from Darcy's divorced but still-feuding parents, to the dastardly pirates, to the younger girlfriend who may be playing both sides. And that's not even counting Darcy and Tom, who begin to doubt their own commitment before a kidnapping forces them to work together and come to terms with their relationship. This is a literal cast of *characters,* and Jennifer brings Big Character Actress Energy to every single moment of Carol Fowler's onscreen time.

In action comedies with a strong element of melodrama like *Shotgun Wedding,* an actor can't be afraid to go *big* in their performance, lest their presence be overwhelmed or outright swallowed up by castmates. Even when she's alerting pirates to the presence of Darcy's multimillionaire father, not realizing he might want to hide from them, Carol does nothing halfway—so who better to play her than an actress known for the same?

However, Jen doesn't play Carol as a caricature but rather as a real person in a scary situation. Carol clearly loves her son and admires her soon-to-be daughter-in-law. She's proud of her success as a Michigan Realtor and unashamed of the powerful sex drive that led the Fowlers to an open relationship. And she is ready and willing to defend her family and her new friends, even if that means using a gun, which she has likely never done before (but then again, Carol is full of surprises, so who knows?). And Jen absolutely nails every moment.

Who doesn't want to watch our girl find her inner badass, protect those she loves, and keep an evil cabal in line? Impeccable timing, a way with a rifle, and the ability to make a mint-green gown and matching hat look like top-designer gear, even when soaking wet—Jennifer has all the makings of an action-comedy star.

## FUN BONUS FACTS

✴ Despite playing his mother in the film, Jennifer is only eleven years older than costar Josh Duhamel.

✴ As Carol, Jennifer sings Edwin McCain's 1990s hit tune "I'll Be," a song that also appeared prominently in one of Jennifer's other films, *A Cinderella Story*.

✴ New besties? While filming, Jennifer Coolidge snuck into her costar Jennifer Lopez's hotel room—and left a video on her phone! Lopez loved it so much that she shared the video on her Instagram on *Shotgun Wedding*'s premiere date.

# Judy Romano

### *We Have a Ghost* (2023)

---

### NOTABLE QUOTABLES

*"Listen, Frank, if you could just fix your little hologram machine, okay?"*

------------

*"I gotta get out of basic cable. It's just so unprofesh."*

---

Judy is *legit*. As cable TV's notorious West Bay Medium, she commands a room, and everyone—including the undead—takes note. With her humongous bright red coif, colorful caftans, and dangling pink jeweled earrings, Judy is ready to up her game, hopefully with a Kardashian or perhaps one of their dearly departed dogs. "No more rest-home readings," she demands. "The food always sucks."

Judy's latest clients are the Presley family, whose house ghost—a man named Ernest (David Harbour) who passed away under unknown circumstances and is only visible to the family's teenaged son Kevin (Jahi Winston)—has turned the Presleys into social media sensations.

Judy is immediately drawn to the Presleys, especially patriarch Frank (Anthony Mackie), who is both a huge fan of her show and very eager to capitalize on the family's newfound fame.

"Nobody said you were cute!" Judy swoons, batting her enormous eyelashes Frank's way. "I just want to know where the wifey is. Lock her up and put her in a box because you're mine."

While Frank is taken with Judy—though not enough to lock up his spouse—Ernest and Kevin are *not* fans of the West Bay Medium and decide to mess with her. At first, Ernest doesn't respond to Judy's entreaties, but then the ghost gives everyone a real show. The house's chandelier starts blinking and swinging. Glass shatters! The cat meows! Doors open and close, and candles flame up! Still unimpressed, Judy comments, "Hey, great production value, Frank."

But Ernest the ghost isn't finished. He moans, groans, and *roars*, frightening the heck out of the camera crew and onlookers. Judy remains unmoved: she checks her makeup while Frank asks Kevin to make Ernest stop the shenanigans. Finally, Ernest makes his way toward Judy—who, like Kevin, can see him—in an *Exorcist*-style contorted position. She says, "On second thought, Tupac was better. I'm gonna fix you in post."

That tears it: Ernest's face melts, and he tries to strangle Judy with *his own entrails*. Judy screams loud enough to wake the dead (oops, too late, he's already awake) and jumps out of the house—through a glass window! Now the Presleys have another viral video—and Judy is gone for good.

While Kevin and Ernest are satisfied with their work, Frank is significantly less so. "They wanted a ghost," he says in frustration, "and we gave them *The Conjuring*!"

## *Why We Heart Judy*

A flamboyant spirit guide who's capitalized on her unique abilities, *and* she smarts off to a big, scary ghost? Judy Romano is a legend. In just one scene she establishes herself as one of *We Have a Ghost*'s most unforgettable characters, spouting off various quotable lines and looking trashily fab while doing so. Tangina from *Poltergeist* could never.

Over the course of her career Jennifer Coolidge has become the go-to for kooky character roles like Judy Romano: big hair, big fashion, and the biggest personality of all. And that's to say nothing about Jennifer's gift for physical comedy, giving each of her characters a memorable presence onscreen. Even if family-friendly ghost movies aren't your bag, *We Have a Ghost* is worth it for Judy Romano alone, thanks to Jen's unparalleled ability to take a few lines of dialogue and turn them into comic gold.

As Judy Romano, Jennifer brings an unforgettable turn to a character who's only briefly onscreen—which is *not* easy to do. Jennifer's natural flamboyance is on full display, and she absolutely nails Judy's funny lines, her obvious lust for the man of the house, and her determination to find the ghost in front of a live audience. Judy won't let her adoring public down, and neither does Jennifer.

### FUN BONUS FACT

✴ Because she does nothing halfway, Jennifer asked costar David Harbour to choke her harder during the climax of their scene.

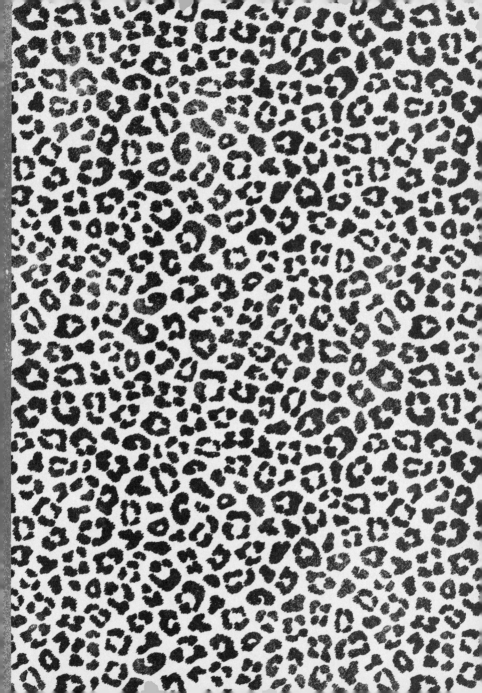

# Epic Guest Star Turns

Every legend starts somewhere, and for Jennifer Coolidge, that was smaller roles on the small screen. Even with just a few lines, Jen can make a tiny part seem like the lead, and her guest spots were only a taste of the stardom to come. Though Jen has appeared in many a show, here's a rundown of her best turns on the most iconic shows in television. And when we say iconic, we mean *Seinfeld, Sex and the City, King of the Hill* . . . the list goes on.

# Jodi

### *Seinfeld* ("The Masseuse," 1993)

Jerry Seinfeld has dated a lot of women, but Jodi is different. First, she's openly unimpressed by his friend George Costanza's (Jason Alexander) disgusting table manners and gender stereotyping (attractive women *do* get traffic tickets—her sister did last week) and won't hug George at the end of their double date. Second, she's a masseuse, even though she refuses to give Jerry a massage, no matter how many dates they have and hints he drops. She'd rather get busy—and is very good at that—which is great for Jerry, but he would love a massage. Jerry remarks that dating a masseuse who won't massage him is "like going to Idaho and eating carrots."

Jodi *does* massage Jerry's pal Kramer (Michael Richards), who says he's "looser than creamed corn" after his appointment. According to Kramer, she sets the mood with New Age ocean sounds and oil and "rubs with love," but Jodi still won't touch Jerry *in that way*. "Why?" Jerry asks. And why, George wonders obsessively, doesn't Jodi like him?

When Jodi comes by with her massage table—she didn't have time to go home after her latest appointment—Jerry tries his best to get it going, but Jodi just can't massage him! Even when Jerry calls her a "massage teaser," Jodi stands her ground. She refuses to like George or to compromise her professional standards—Jerry, don't ever call her again.

## Why We Heart Jodi

Gotta love a woman with boundaries! Jodi knows exactly who she is—a professional masseuse who doesn't take any guff from the men in her life. Though she only appeared in one episode—sorry, George—Jodi introduced the gift that is Jennifer Coolidge to the world. Jennifer positively shines as the masseuse—whose character gives the episode its title—who *knows* she can't mess up her career for a man. She keeps up with comic giant Jerry Seinfeld and film, TV, and stage actor Jason Alexander, matching them quip for quip without missing a beat. And as always, her comic timing is impeccable.

Though Jennifer had studied and performed extensively for years, her role on *Seinfeld* was life-changing. As Jennifer told *Radio & TV Talk* in 2009, "The minute I was on that show, I was able to support myself just acting. It opened so many doors."

### FUN BONUS FACT

✦ Jennifer was cast in *Seinfeld*—and, on the same day, the sketch show *SheTV*—right as her mother was dying of pancreatic cancer. She told E. Alex Jung of *Vulture*, "My mother's last words to me were, like, 'I can't believe it.' . . . But she was thrilled because she didn't think anything was going to happen."

# Miss Kremzer

*King of the Hill* ("Plastic White Female,"
"Leanne's Saga," "Propane Boom," and
"Wings of the Dope," 1997–1999)

---

### NOTABLE QUOTABLES

*"Very good, Sharona. If this hair weren't attached to a
horse's rear end, I'd swear it was Cher's."*

-----------

*"And that's why blondes don't necessarily have more fun!"*

---

Miss Kremzer is the brunette-hair-rocking, sensible-blue-cardigan-sporting, cat-eye-glasses-on-a-chain-wearing, most *terrifying* teacher Arlen Beauty Academy has ever seen. She's really more of a headmistress: neat as a pin and completely intimidating in the name of good hair. And she has it out for crop-topped, trembling first-year student Luanne Platter (Brittany Murphy). Luanne thinks "beauty is an art." Miss Kremzer begs to differ.

After her plastic practice head is caught in a compromising position and subsequently destroyed, Luanne cuts the hair of her uncle Hank Hill (Mike Judge) for her final exam, but Miss Kremzer fails a devastated Luanne. When Hank expresses how much he loves the haircut, Miss Kremzer reverses the grade to passing and remembers the most important part of a beautician's career: repeat business and referrals.

We next see Miss Kremzer on Arlen Beauty Academy's Mother-Daughter Night, when Luanne brings her mother Leanne, recently released from prison after stabbing Luanne's dad with a fork—except Leanne doesn't show up. Miss Kremzer is *très* unsurprised.

The next semester Miss Kremzer reminds Luanne that she *must* pass the hair-dyeing exam to qualify for her final year of school. So what if Luanne's boyfriend, Buckley, just blew up (literally) and her classmates don't believe in her? No excuses at the Arlen Beauty Academy.

Despite a misguided vision of her boyfriend's guardian angel and a sleep-deprived car wreck involving a Wiener Wagon, Luanne doesn't pass. But inspired by Buckley's winged spirit, she gets a tuition refund from Miss Kremzer and enrolls in the local community college instead. Kremzer who?

## Why We Heart Miss Kremzer

This beauty school owner and operator is the ultimate taskmaster. Her relentless quest for perfection—even if it's just dyeing the tails of horses and making sure everyone submits their three-hundred-dollar tuition checks on time—is an ideal fit for the ambitious young stylists of Arlen, Texas, who just want to do the hair of the girls who work at the pretzel stand at the mall. Miss Kremzer reminds her students that a bad haircut can cost a client their job or get them beat up, which is why they practice on the elderly. But she instructs the students not to say anything bad because some of them can hear you. Despite her strict nature, Miss Kremzer just wants her aspiring stylist pupils to succeed. (Probably.) After all, in beauty school, as in life, "You only get one head."

At this point in her career, Jennifer was slowly but surely making a name for herself thanks to her excellent sense of comedy and character; her unique, bubbly voice; and her expressive face and physicality. But with a voice-over role like Miss Kremzer, Jennifer could only rely on two of those three. Lesser performers would have faltered, but not our girl. Using only her voice, Jen brought Arlen, Texas's strict brunette schoolmarm to life. Miss Kremzer didn't get to where she was by being *nice*, and Jennifer turned a four-episode stint into an iconic performance in Mike Judge's unforgettable series. She also kicked off a new facet of her career, later appearing in other animated series and films. Hank Hill doesn't interact much with Miss Kremzer, but there's no doubt he would give Jennifer his highest endorsement: a hearty *yup!*

# Frederica

*Frasier* **("Forgotten but Not Gone," 2001)**

**NOTABLE QUOTABLES**

*"Oh, it's just your leg I'm pulling!"*

Frederica is the new substitute physical therapist for Frasier's father, Martin Crane (John Mahoney), while his regular therapist, Daphne, is away. Frederica is aware that patients slack off on their regular exercises for reasons like holidays and death, but as she tells Frasier (Kelsey Grammer) and Martin, "There is only one excuse I accept: holidays!" Her joking demeanor quickly gives way to a bossy attitude—"You show me your exercise mat, now!" she orders Martin in her thick German accent—as well as a distinctive walk (let's just say it's chest first).

Initially, Frederica is *not* amused by Martin's physical state, declaring him "shamefully out of shape," but she vows to change that quickly. Off camera, Martin is also not amused with the paces his substitute PT puts him through, and the audience can hear him screaming in protest. Later, while enjoying delicious German cooking and a stein of lager—the latter homemade by none other than Frederica's papa—Martin recalls his tough afternoon, saying, "She did things to me . . ." Frederica emerges, saying good food is earned with exercise, but when Frasier reaches for Martin's plate, she retaliates with a hard slap to the face and a declaration: "You haven't earned it!" Of course, Frederica is only joking.

## Why We Heart Frederica

Frederica may be a taskmaster, but she knows what it takes to get Martin, who has suffered a stroke, back up to fighting speed. The secret to Frederica's success? A fantastic supper and the biggest stein of beer Martin Crane can handle. And of course, she'll share with his son.

*Frasier* ran for eleven seasons—truly a jaw-dropping tenure—and was known for its stellar cast: not only Kelsey Grammer, who'd made a name for himself *and* Frasier Crane on a little series called *Cheers*, but also stage and screen legends John Mahoney, who played Frasier's dad, and David Hyde Pierce, who played Frasier's brother, Niles.

Still early in her acting career, Jennifer shared scenes with Grammer and Mahoney, making the absolute most of her short time onscreen by providing a sharp contrast to both Frasier's deadpan bemusement and Martin's dry humor. It's no wonder Jen reigned supreme over TV guest-star roles in the late nineties and early aughts. If you can hold your own with Jerry Seinfeld and Kelsey Grammer, you can do anything.

# Victoria

### *Sex and the City* ("The Perfect Present," 2003)

Victoria will *not* let her recent breakup bring her down, especially after six Advil on an empty stomach didn't kill her. The glaringly obvious solution? Lose ten pounds, kick the Zoloft, and kick-*start* a brand-spanking-new career in designing purses. As Victoria says, "Because of that fucker, I've discovered I'm Fendi."

So what if Victoria doesn't have a storefront, a customer base, or any real sense of taste that we can see? Who needs *any* of that when you can guilt your friends into coming to your apartment for a purse party? Especially old friends like New York's favorite sex columnist.

"Look at this one—little shoes!" Victoria exclaims as she presents a less-than-gorgeous handbag for the perusal of the always-impeccably-styled Carrie Bradshaw (Sarah Jessica Parker). Among the less-than-pretty offerings are a small bag with plastic fruit and a pink sparkly purse with hot-pink feathers and fringe everywhere. At least the tuna tartlets are delicious and the champagne is free—all the better to mill around in the ruins of Victoria's relationship. As Carrie quietly observes to her friends, "Ladies, these aren't bags. They're bagg*age!*"

Unfortunately for Victoria, this purse party's about to take an interesting turn. Unbeknownst to New York's latest emotionally fragile purse designer, she's hired a staff of cater waiters that includes Smith "Jerry" Jerrod (Jason Lewis), the waiter that Carrie's best friend Samantha Jones (Kim Cattrall) shared a white-hot night with not long ago after meeting him at the hot new restaurant Raw. After catching Samantha and Jerry *in* the raw next to the extra dishes and champagne bottles, Victoria proclaims, "I'm way too fucking fragile to see this!" and proceeds to kick *all* the partygoers out of her apartment *tout suite*. Good thing Carrie and company have dinner reservations.

## Why We Heart Victoria

Gotta love a girlboss. In her tight black dress, silver and turquoise lariat necklace, and straightened hair, wronged woman Victoria is determined to make the best of a breakup—and hopefully a little moolah. She's not afraid of sacrifice; after all, she cut up her bedspread to craft a fuzzy, bright purple bag. And when the party's over, it's *over*: Victoria even throws over a whole rack of her handmade purses to make a point. Can't say she's not decisive.

*Sex and the City* was one of the best series of the early aughts, with a veritable Who's Who of actors making guest appearances. So of course our girl Jen got in there, with a fantastically funny character to boot. In only one scene Jennifer makes quite the impression—from her maniacally smiling beginning to her screaming-at-the-guests end. Now *that's* the mark of a star.

Jennifer was a perfect match for *Sex and the City*, flawlessly combining Victoria's daffy downtown optimism with a healthy dose of snark. Tottering around on high heels and hawking handmade handbags as the Fab Four look on in amusement, Jennifer simultaneously elevates the humorous scene and delivers down-home belly laughs as Victoria slowly but surely unravels. Is there *anything* Jennifer Coolidge can't do?

## FUN BONUS FACT

* According to interviews, Jennifer was originally cast as Lexi Featherston, the aging party girl who falls out a high-rise window in the sixth-season episode "Splat!". Kristen Johnston ended up in the role, while Jennifer was given the part of Victoria.

# Amanda Buffamonteezi

## *Friends* ("The One with Ross's Tan," 2003)

Amanda's reputation precedes her: she's the subject of much discussion between Phoebe (Lisa Kudrow) and Monica (Courteney Cox). Amanda lived in the same building as the friends before Chandler (Matthew Perry) moved in. Now, she's moved back from England, where she's picked up both an insufferable fake British accent, even though she's from Yonkers, and a propensity to brag about celebrities she's spotted— or, er, done more with. As an unimpressed Phoebe points out, however, Amanda may have slept with Billy Joel, but who hasn't?

What's worse, Amanda *won't stop calling* now that she's back stateside. Phoebe and Monica decide to ghost Amanda until she gets the hint, a plan that quickly goes awry when Chandler picks up the phone and Monica is pressured to invite Amanda to dinner. To get them out of it, Chandler promises to call with an "emergency": he and Phoebe's husband, Mike, have been in a car accident, and Monica and Phoebe must go to them.

When Amanda finally makes an appearance, she does not disappoint. She blows into Central Perk with the confidence that only a faux Brit can have. Her big, bright blonde hair, trench coat, and heels cause quite the stir—and that's before she shows off her strappy black dress

and proclaims, "Look how young I look!" After entreating the women to touch her abs ("I don't exercise at all") and smell her neck ("It's my natural scent"), Amanda recalls a time gone by. In 1992 Amanda was sleeping with Evel Knievel and Phoebe was the one ghosting *Monica*. The call from Chandler comes just in time, but a now-irritated Monica says that Mike has *not* been in the car accident, so now Phoebe is stuck.

Phoebe drags Amanda back to the apartment to confront Monica. Of course, Amanda comments that her "flat is twice this size" and tells Chandler he looks "positively ghastly." A guilty Monica and Phoebe decide to give Amanda another chance—only to find her jumping around for a befuddled Chandler. "Can you believe it?" she asks him. "I've never had any professional dance training!"

## *Why We Heart Amanda*

Amanda is a trench-coated truth teller with confidence to spare. She's eager to reconnect with her "friends"—even when they try to dodge her enthusiastic calls—and she owns who she is, from her put-upon dialect to her pretty hair to her high heels. Plus, as Chandler says, "That fake British woman's a real bitch, but she sure can dance!"

The role of Amanda was a wonderful opportunity for Jennifer to show off her entire skill set to a huge audience. Millions of people watched and delighted in her one-of-a-kind delivery and style, fantastic physical comedy, and delightfully *un*real dialect. Jennifer joined the ranks of *Friends'* legions of legendary guests—including her *Legally Blonde* costar Reese Witherspoon. And though she wasn't a big name just *yet*, all signs pointed to success.

### FUN BONUS FACT

✦ You never get a second chance to make a first impression, and our girl took that to heart. After *Friends* ended, Jen was cast in her first major television role on the *Friends* spinoff, *Joey*. Jennifer played Bobbie Morganstern, wannabe actor Joey Tribbiani's (Matt LeBlanc) quirky Los Angeles agent, for two seasons and forty-six episodes.

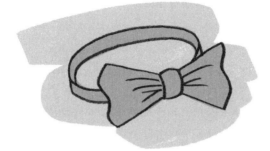

# Bobbie St. Brown

*Party Down* ("James Rolf High School Twentieth Reunion" and "Stennheiser-Pong Wedding Reception," 2009)

### NOTABLE QUOTABLES

*"Did you know dolphins can change a baby's diapers underwater?"*

Thinking of giving up your acting career and moving back home with your parents? Never fear, Bobbie St. Brown is here! Bobbie rocks a sassy French twist and black pencil skirt with her pink bow tie and is subbing for her roommate Constance (Jane Lynch)—whom she once hit with her car when they were up for the same role in *Cannonball Run II*, then gifted her a copy of *Zen and the Art of Motorcycle Maintenance*—as Party Down Catering works an eventful twenty-year high school reunion and a power-gay wedding reception.

What's more, Bobbie heard that cater waiter and series protagonist Henry (Adam Scott) is about to quit acting for good—but if he listens to the dolphin sounds she has on her Walkman and smiles fifty times a day (but not ninety, because that would make a person insane), she *knows* he'll keep on trucking.

When it's time for the outdoor wedding reception, Bobbie is incredibly excited about the possibility of an Elton John appearance (it *is* a gay wedding, after all!). Even the surprise presence of the evil, black-clad Valhalla Catering staff and their petite but terrifying manager, Uta (Kristen Bell), who Bobbie affectionately calls "a little elf in the woods" and who is determined to keep Party Down behind the scenes at all costs, does nothing to temper Bobbie's boundless positivity.

Thanks to the psilocybin mushrooms she downed before the ceremony, as she always does while in nature, it's going to be a *magical* evening. What better time to rejoice in the presence of a bowl of "sun eggs" (lemons), help oneself to a glass of champagne, and ask the two grooms, "How can you tell if a guy is gay?"

## *Why We Heart Bobbie*

Her relentless—and we do mean *relentless*—optimism! For Bobbie, life is all about second chances. After all, who else hits their professional rival with their car, then befriends and moves in with them? While the rest of the Party Down staff can be jaded and snarky, tired of passing appetizers and pouring white wine for the rich, entitled LA elite, Bobbie St. Brown is just genuinely happy to be there (with or without psychedelics, though they certainly help). Plus, two words: dolphin calls.

Jen had some big shoes to fill with this guest spot. As Bobbie St. Brown, she "replaced" her *Best in Show* costar and good friend Jane Lynch, who, as Constance, was a main cast member in season one of *Party Down*. Rather than trying to *be* Constance, with her dry delivery and anecdotes that bordered on unbelievable, Jennifer brought her own energy to Bobbie, Constance's pal and roommate, who, as it turns out, is a natural fit for the motley cater waiter crew. Jennifer's presence is unmistakable. Rather than sneak up on you, she's truly "in your face," and you can't ignore her.

Jennifer Coolidge was a perfect fit for zany Bobbie, who never met a boundary she wouldn't cross in the most delightful way possible. And when Bobbie ingests magic mushrooms to make a wedding reception more interesting for all involved, Jennifer plays the drug trip for all its hilarious worth. *Party Down* recently enjoyed a successful reboot—please bring back Jen for season two, if she's not too busy.

# Whitney S. Pierce

*Glee* ("What the World Needs Now" and "A Wedding," 2015)

Whitney S. Pierce is the mother of McKinley High Cheerio and New Directions dancing *legend* Brittany S. Pierce (Heather Morris). Before Brittany announces her engagement to former Cheerio and New Directions alum Santana Lopez (Naya Rivera), Whitney and her husband, Pierce Pierce (Ken Jeong), have some big news for their daughter. Turns out, there's a reason Brittany is a mathematical genius, even though Whitney is of average intelligence and Pierce is below average in that department (he has an IQ of 60 and is only suited to growing vegetables).

After a misunderstanding on Whitney and Pierce's honeymoon in London, she ended up having a one-night stand with the legendary physicist Dr. Stephen Hawking. Oh, by the way, Whitney is *thrilled* about Brittany's engagement.

Whitney is equally psyched when Brittany agrees to hold the wedding in the Indiana barn where Brittany was born. Whitney and Pierce were on a trip to Amish country when Whitney suddenly felt horrible indigestion from all the apple butter. She ran into a barn to go to the bathroom but actually was in labor. Upon Brittany's birth, Whitney swaddled the new baby in a stray Mr. Submarine wrapper and presented her to a shocked and joyful Pierce.

Whitney keeps Pierce from embarrassing himself and others during Brittany and Santana's wedding toast. Plus, she comes clean about Brittany's parentage and birth and is genuinely excited for her daughter to marry another woman. And finally, Whitney looks incredible at the reception, rocking a fitted, red-fringed frock, dancing for her life, and singing "I'm So Excited" with Santana's mother, Maribel Lopez (Gloria Estefan). Now *that's* a great mom.

## Why We Heart Whitney

Can we say *perfect casting*? Heather Morris infused the character of Brittany with slammin' dance moves and a healthy dose of sweet weirdness. Who better to play the woman who birthed her in an Indiana barn and later rocks out at her gay wedding than Jennifer Coolidge?

*Glee* was a smash hit and a cultural phenomenon, running for six seasons, selling out stadium tours, and teaching the world about inclusivity and the power of music.

With her delightful delivery and gift for rocking a tight red dress while singing a 1980s hit, there was no better mother figure for Brittany than Jen. In just two episodes Jennifer made quite the impression: taking over an Indiana barn, revealing Brittany's true parentage and truly amazing birth story, and sending her beloved daughter off in style in an epic double wedding. Thanks to Jennifer Coolidge, the "S" of Whitney's middle initial might as well stand for *star*.

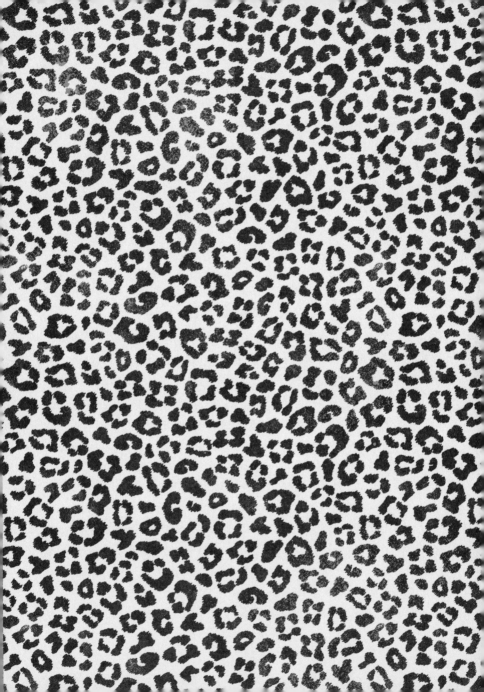

# Small Screen Success Stories

When it comes to TV, guest spots are one challenge, but recurring and lead characters are quite another. How exactly *does* one make their mark over and over again? Look no further than Jennifer Coolidge's featured television roles—leading up to the biggest one of all at an exclusive resort in Maui . . .

# Bobbie Morganstern

## *Joey* (2004–2006)

---

### NOTABLE QUOTABLES

*"I'd like to keep that little piece of chicken in my pocket and snack on him all day."*

------------

*"Did I not tell you? I'm a little off. I was at the gate looking through my purse for my wallet, and I accidentally Tasered myself."*

------------

*"There is nothing that I wouldn't do for you! I'd throw on a meat skirt and wrestle a lion! I'd pull off my own ears and eat them!"*

---

After Joey Tribbiani (Matt LeBlanc) leaves New York, Central Perk, and his loving group of *Friends*, he goes to the logical next stop for any aspiring film and television actor: Los Angeles, California. Too bad his new television gig is *immediately* canceled. But Joey's agent, Roberta "Bobbie" Morganstern, is there to help him attain fame and fortune. Or, at least, she'll try . . . as soon as she stops mistaking Joey for Tori Spelling and offering him a cover model gig for *Brides* magazine.

Early on, Bobbie assures her new client, "I know how to deal with crazy actors. You just smile and tell them what they wanna hear." When Joey asks, "So can you help me?" Bobbie puts on a big—possibly fake—smile and says, "Absolutely!" Gotta love an agent with scruples.

Bobbie is a self-proclaimed "superagent" and, according to *Entertainment Weekly*, the twelfth most powerful woman in Hollywood. She's so powerful that, at one point, Phil Collins even sued her. Powerful or not, Bobbie's looking for love . . . namely, in the form of Michael Tribbiani (Paulo Costanzo), Joey's roommate and twenty-year-old nephew, a sheltered aerospace engineer who's incredibly nervous around women. Eventually, Bobbie hires Michael's mother and Joey's sister, hairstylist Gina (Drea de Matteo), as her secretary; after all, the two share a brash, funny personality.

Aggressive and ever-so-slightly ditzy, Bobbie makes her own fun in and out of the office. She isn't above making her assistant do silly tricks for Bobbie's amusement or even using a stun gun on herself. Soon after the latter happens, Joey shares with Bobbie his aspiration to make an Oscar speech, at which Bobbie laughs heartily and responds, "Oscar? Did you get Tasered too?" And soon after *that*, Bobbie has yet another run-in with the Taser: "I think, on some level, I may be doing it on purpose."

Bobbie is known not just for her brutal honesty with clients—she candidly informs Joey that "Italians are out this year. It may be time for you to call in your boy band connections," before learning that Joey was not, in fact, in a boy band—but also for her depth of knowledge about Hollywood. She describes a potential new audition for Joey like this: "Well, it's a sexy new nighttime drama set in a mountain resort. It's called *Deep Powder*. It's *Baywatch* on skis, and it's the dumbest script I ever read. It's gonna be huge!" And what do you know, Joey ends up booking it—though he gets fired due to Bobbie's outrageous demands.

More than anything, Bobbie will go to the mat for her clients. When Joey calls her because he's gotten in a bad situation, before hearing any details, Bobbie is ready to go. "Okay, here's the game plan," she tells her client. "Flush the drugs, throw the gun in the river, we'll tell everyone it was exhaustion."

Best. Agent. Ever?

## Why We Heart Bobbie

Being Hollywood's twelfth most powerful woman is a veritable pressure cooker, but when she's not on the wrong side of a stun gun, Bobbie handles it all in style. And because appearance is everything in Los Angeles, she looks great. Her blonde, flowing hair would make a mermaid jealous (when it's not in a fabulous bouffant, that is), and her blazers are always just barely buttoned. It's no wonder she's never starved for male companionship.

Jennifer played Bobbie in the *Joey* pilot thinking it would just be a onetime shot, but when the series went to air, Bobbie was kept as a recurring character. When the show was renewed for a second season, Bobbie was given a bigger role. And no wonder: with Jennifer's vibrant ability to create and maintain distinctive characters like Bobbie, who *wouldn't* give her more screen time? Seems like the powers that be had the same thought as the rest of us: the more Jennifer on our screens, the better.

Playing Bobbie was a way for Jennifer to gift us all with a sustained presence on television and kick off her slow-but-steady ascent into the TV stratosphere. Jennifer infused Bobbie with her signature big blonde hair, inherent sass, and ability to make each and every scene her own.

Even though *Joey* only lasted for two seasons, the show—and super-agent Bobbie Morganstern—had a huge impact on Jennifer's career. Other main and recurring TV roles would follow, including the one that many years later would launch Jennifer onto the A list. Hint: it involves an exclusive resort, a suite named after fruit, and an urn full of ashes.

## FUN BONUS FACTS

✳ Though the show wasn't a *Friends*-level hit, Matt LeBlanc was a hit with Jennifer. In a 2009 interview with the *Atlanta Journal-Constitution*, she described LeBlanc as "So nice. Such a good guy." How *you* doin', indeed.

✳ This wouldn't be the last time Jennifer played a character named Bobbie. A few years after *Joey*'s cancellation, she appeared on two episodes of *Party Down* as Bobbie St. Brown (see page 79). *Party Down*'s Bobbie was a bit more like Joey Tribbiani—an actress struggling to make ends meet between auditions and having wacky adventures along the way—but of course both Bobbies have Jennifer's signature style and spot-on comedic delivery.

# Betty Boykewich

### *The Secret Life of the*
### *American Teenager* (2008–2012)

---

### NOTABLE QUOTABLES

*"Hating yourself, it's just a big waste of time."*

- - - - - - - - - - - -

*"Not only can you buy me breakfast, but you can buy me,*
*'cause I'm that kind of girl!"*

---

Sweet Betty is introduced as the love interest for Leo "Sausage King" Boykewich (Steve Schirripa), a widowed butcher shop owner. Betty's origins are a bit seedier than most, as she was very recently a "lady of the night." Betty was hired as an escort by local young man Tom Bowman (Luke Zimmerman), who has Down syndrome, though the two only spend the night talking. And though Leo's teenaged son, Ben (Kenny Baumann), at first resents Betty's presence in his father's life, Betty wins him over with her honesty about her past and genuine kindness.

Leo proposes to Betty, but there's a major hiccup: Betty reveals that she may still be married to someone else. Upon finding out that Betty's former husband has died, Betty and Leo wed in a ceremony fit for a queen. Later, Leo suspects that his assistant may be in love with him and considers ending his marriage to Betty, but eventually *Betty* asks for a divorce and Leo agrees. Betty decides she wants to pursue her own dreams by attending college. You go, girl: get that bachelor's degree and never look back!

## *Why We Heart Betty*

"Hooker with a heart of gold" is a beloved trope for a reason, and as always, Jennifer plays the character to perfection—never judging Betty but instead infusing the character with an inherent sweetness. Betty makes the best use out of her services when Tom retains her for the evening, providing him with a listening ear. When Betty begins dating Leo, Ben is judgmental at first, but Betty perseveres.

Later, when Ben's wife, Adrian (Francia Raisa), loses their baby to a miscarriage, Betty consoles her. Adrian says, "You're the first person who hasn't treated me like I'm going to break." "Honey, you're already broken," Betty reassures the traumatized young woman. "What you went through, I mean, it shatters people, and you just have to put all the pieces back together."

*The Secret Life of the American Teenager* ran for five seasons. Beginning with the surprise pregnancy of fifteen-year-old Amy Juergens (Shailene Woodley), the series was rife with hookups, breakups, and failed engagements, more than one unexpected baby, and full-blown angst in every episode. At its heart, the show was a melodrama—emphasis on the *drama*. In a cast of mostly teenaged characters who constantly break up, make up, and fall in love all over again with one another, a special actress was needed to bring empathy, compassion, and a grounding force to the ensemble.

Enter Jennifer Coolidge, who knows exactly how to turn words on a page into a fully realized human being by infusing each character with feeling, bringing humor to every line, and letting honesty shine through every gesture. Though Betty's arc is just as chaotic as everyone else's and her background is initially considered "less than" by some—including her own stepson—Betty is kind to everyone she encounters. She's unapologetic about who she was, who she is, and who she will become. Basically, Betty Boykewich is *goals*, and she's surely gonna kick butt at college. And by playing Betty as a real person, Jennifer kicked absolute butt in this role.

## FUN BONUS FACT

✴ Jennifer played stepmother Fiona in the original *A Cinderella Story* (2004). Later, her *Secret Life* castmate Megan Park played one of the stepsisters in 2011's *A Cinderella Story: Once Upon a Song*.

# Sophie Kachinsky

## *2 Broke Girls* (2012–2017)

---

### NOTABLE QUOTABLES

*"I once had sex on a bus and I was driving it.
Oh . . . were those kids late to school."*

------------

*"Uh oh, I think it's getting too real in here for me.
I'm gonna go push up my boobs and glue my tooth back on!"*

------------

*"Oh, spring is in the air. This is the time of year in
Poland when the snow would melt and all our dead
relatives would float back to us."*

---

Sophie Kachinsky is the resident of apartment 2G, moving in after the previous tenant dies, and she is the neighbor to the series' titular "two broke girls": ex-delinquent Max Black (Kat Dennings) and ex-socialite Caroline Channing (Beth Behrs), who've bonded while working minimum-wage restaurant jobs in Brooklyn and hope to launch their own cupcake business.

Though they first mistake Sophie for a madam, the older woman immediately takes to Max and Caroline, always greeting them with a hearty, "Hi girls!" even in the "quiet room" at a spa. Once she knows where they work, she's always up for visiting the Williamsburg Diner, even staking out her own booth. When asked how many are in her party, Sophie retorts, "What kind of question is that? I am my own party!" Truer words have never been spoken.

Sophie loves to visit the Williamsburg Diner for many reasons. First, her sweet neighbor girls work there. Second, she can always show off today's look, often topped off by a bright fur stole tied with a big bow. Third—and perhaps most importantly—there are *men* at this diner, and there is nothing Sophie loves more than a man . . . or three. Sure, she often mistakes diner owner Han (Matthew Moy) for a woman or a child, but Sophie is most fond of cashier Earl (Garrett Morris), who can match her flirtatious banter quip for quip.

"If you looked any sweeter, you'd fire up my diabetes!" Earl observes one night when Sophie teeters in. "Oh, Earl!" Sophie drawls in her thick Polish accent. "You wouldn't be the first man to lose a limb over me!" At another point, Earl greets Sophie, clad in bright yellow, with a "Well, well, well, here comes the sun, and the moon looks great too!" Sophie adores the nuanced compliment, replying, "Oh, Earl, your flirting is just the right amount of dirty, and that's not easy!" Don't ship these two just yet, though.

Best of all, Sophie finds *luv* at the Williamsburg Diner in the tall and lanky form of short-order cook Oleg (Jonathan Kite), who she eventually marries. The two have sizzling chemistry, which they put to good use in Sophie's bedroom. The couple "use a ball and chain in their lovemaking," according to Sophie. They also enjoy sensual oils, though, as Sophie informs Caroline and Max, not peppermint because "it makes his tongue swell, and you know his tongue is the best part about him."

Oleg texts Sophie original erotic haikus, and Sophie returns the favor with naughty images involving a Dustbuster . . . when she's not accidentally texting them to her grandfather in Poland, that is.

Speaking of Poland, Sophie is proud of her heritage—and her brother's club foot—but relieved to leave her homeland behind. Likely, immigration was a relief after engaging in extreme fighting as a young lady: "They would throw a big hunk of cheese in a trough and let the girls go at it!" Once Sophie made enough money in the United States, she purchased her tiny hometown, only to burn it to the ground. Hey, they had it coming for not letting her be a cheerleader. Also, Sophie warns the two broke girls of a Polish superstition she still holds dear: "Be careful. A cat is not always a cat. . . . In Poland we believe if you die outside, you're reincarnated as a cat."

Sophie is fond of sharing bits and pieces from her past. For example, according to Sophie, there is a very special holiday in the Polish community known as Duza Day: when a Polish girl grows to six feet tall, everyone throws her a huge party. "Mine happened when I was seven!" Sophie proudly discloses.

Over six seasons Sophie develops the much-beloved catchphrase "I'll be in my booth!" This refers to her regular booth at the Williamsburg Diner. But don't worry: if you sit in it by mistake, Sophie will gently but firmly make it right. Sophie states to a family who've made that error—while moving their plates of food to another table—"Well, this is weird. . . . It's okay. You didn't know. Don't let it happen again. Okay, bye bye now!"

# *Why We Heart Sophie*

In a word, Sophie Kachinsky is *colorful*. It's not unusual for her to answer the door clad in a majestic, brightly colored caftan embellished with mohair, wielding a fruit-studded cocktail in a pretty glass. She favors vivid hues like red and yellow, as well as vibrant pastels like lavender (she pairs the latter with a fetching parasol to match). Sophie's long, blonde hair is always perfectly curled and parted to the side, her bosoms are pushed to the heavens, and even her gym shoes are a pair of sparkly stilettos. (Her favorite store below 14th Street is called Rhinestoned.)

Like the gift she is, Sophie loves wearing ribbons and bows tied in her hair, festooned on her tight frocks, and closing up her beloved fur stoles. #glamlife. Also, #goals.

Sophie is a flawless foil to Max and Caroline. While Max and Caroline sport Williamsburg Diner uniforms of mustard yellow and ketchup red (*eww*), Sophie forever shines in flamboyant fashions. While the two broke girls are out there trying to make their cupcake-shop dreams a reality and doing their best to get out of the "broke girl" box, Sophie is living her best life and enjoying every minute.

She's also living the dream as an entrepreneur. Though Sophie was a nurse back in Poland—"You hear of Doctors Without Borders? We were nurses without credentials!"—she now runs a successful cleaning service, the aptly named Sophie's Choice. "They clean like their life depends on it!" crows a blurb in *Manhattan* magazine. (Okay, so maybe she's not going to receive a World's Best Boss coffee mug anytime soon.)

We love Jennifer as Sophie because who else could play Brooklyn's loudest, horniest, and most colorful resident with such aplomb? *2 Broke Girls* graced the world with multiple seasons of Jen doing what Jen does best: playing the ultimate character. Because Jennifer is so good, there are countless incredible Sophie moments over the course of the series, but two moments in particular stand out. First, when Caroline prepares for a date, Sophie presents her with a grab bag of condoms in various sizes—Sophie calls the smallest one "he's got a great personality."

And the second is when Max is having trouble sleeping, Sophie is all too happy to choose just the right meds from her spice rack . . . which is actually a pill rack. ("You gotta cook me dinner sometime!" Max remarks.) "I never use them," Sophie says of sleeping pills. "I just need three hours of sleep during the night and six during the day!" However, Sophie cautions Max against the German pills, which should only be taken "in case they release the bombs, or I'm ever abandoned in space!" Sophie also demonstrates then and there how *not* to lose a pill in one's ample cleavage.

Could anyone *but* Jennifer Coolidge have delivered this combo of hilarious dialogue, physical comedy, and interaction with other performers—in a flamboyant accent and a low-cut costume, no less? I think we all know the answer to that. She's more than a little unconventional, but Jennifer as Sophie Kachinsky absolutely *rules*. She's a brightly clad, impeccably coiffed, extremely libertine reminder to the girls that there *is* life after brokeness, thankless jobs, and unluckiness in love.

Caroline often says, "It's just Sophie," when 2G's most dazzling resident shows up at her door, but thanks to Jennifer's brilliant performance, what could have been a live-action cartoon character is instead one of the funniest supporting characters in sitcom history. It's no wonder the studio audience often greets Sophie—and Jennifer—with a hearty *"Woo!"*

## FUN BONUS FACTS

✳ Both Beth Behrs (Caroline Channing) and Jennifer have appeared in *American Pie* films. Beth was a cast member of 2009's *American Pie Presents: The Book of Love*, and of course, Jennifer kicked off the franchise (and made several follow-up appearances) as the MILF herself, Stifler's Mom.

✳ Next stop: the Super Bowl. On the biggest night of television, Jennifer appeared as Sophie Kachinsky in an ad known as the "2 Broke Girls Spectacular Super Bowl Commercial." This wouldn't be Jen's last time at the Super Bowl: in 2023 she and Mike White would team up for an ad campaign!

# Karen Calhoun

### *The Watcher* (2022)

## NOTABLE QUOTABLES

*"Eat a d\*ck, Stephanie!"*

------------

*"He sucked. He really did. He was a real, like, p\*ssy and he couldn't, like, make his junk work."*

------------

*"My napkin smells like vinegar."*

Karen Calhoun is a *go-getter*. She wears tight power suits. She plays tennis with a competitive edge that would intimidate Billie Jean King. She talks openly about her sex life—including past lovers' anatomy—and she doesn't give a damn if it makes anyone uncomfortable.

Most importantly, Karen Calhoun is devoted to making suburban real estate dreams come true—by any means necessary—through her position at Darren Dunn Realty. Karen is *thrilled* when her art school friend Nora Brannock (Naomi Watts) shows up to town with her husband (Bobby Cannavale) and two teenagers at the very house Karen is showing. She knows the area's hottest property would be perfect for her old pal and her brood, who are looking for a change from their city dwelling. After all, according to Karen, "New York City will be underwater in, like, five years."

But after the family moves in, they learn their new home has a mysterious "watcher" who sends threatening letters. Luckily, Nora has Karen, who's *always* up for tennis and lunch at the country club and happily fills Nora in on all the town gossip, as well as the intimate details of her terrible ex, Rick Bluck, whose *anatomy* didn't always function, and her unnamed new paramour, who is giving Karen the best you-know-what *ever*. (Nora didn't really ask, but Karen, being Karen, is undeterred.) Karen urges Nora to keep the spark going with her own husband—see, she *is* a helpful friend.

Back at the Brannocks', things are going less than swimmingly. The watcher's threats are escalating, leaving the family no choice but to camp out at a hotel, and local law enforcement, led by the charismatic Detective Chamberland (Christopher McDonald), isn't interested in pursuing the leads provided by the family's newly hired private detective. A very concerned Karen urges Nora to sell, even showing her a new house. When Nora hesitates to list her home, Karen doesn't give up.

Soon, the truth comes out: Karen owns the LLC that has its eye on the Brannocks' house. Karen's also in cahoots with Detective Chamberland (the giver of the good, *ahem*, Karen mentioned earlier to Nora). And bless her crafty little heart, after the Brannocks move back to the city, Karen Calhoun's nefarious plan to nab the hot property *finally works*.

In the end, the manipulator in pink fur, who never met a spiked heel or floral print she didn't love, gets exactly what she wants. Now "a single woman taking care of herself," as Karen snobbishly declares to her interior decorating team—Detective Chamberland is history—she rebuffs baked goods from the oddball neighbors (Margo Martindale and Mia Farrow). After all, Karen Calhoun couldn't possibly cheat on her keto diet.

But when the sun goes down, things get a little hairy. Karen receives a creepy call, her bathtub overfills at an alarming rate, and her dog is nowhere to be found. She calls Detective Chamberland, but her rebuffed lover is of no help. Finally, Karen finds her dog—no longer of this world—and after she spots a scary hooded figure, Karen Calhoun is last seen running down the middle of the road screaming, her silk robe majestically flapping behind her and her furry mules click-clacking away into the night.

## Why We Heart Karen

Karen is the very type of hustler that has inspired a Jay-Z hit. She's not always nice—in fact, "nice" is the last word anyone would use to describe her. (When you think about it, Karen Calhoun may in fact be the definitive *Karen*.) However, as Karen knows, you can't make an omelet

without breaking a few eggs—or, in her case, selling a house that is under a stalker's surveillance.

Karen also *speaks her mind*, even when it's not the sweetest words coming out of her perfectly lipsticked mouth. She's bitchy, she's horny, and she's here to sell you a house and possibly steal your man along the way. Karen Calhoun isn't afraid to drop the f-bomb on the country club tennis court, openly trash her ex in the country club's dining room, or get certain art school friends booted from said country club.

And when flipping Nora's house under the guise of a shady LLC would be *far* more profitable than just letting her friend and her family live their lives, Karen keeps pushing the issue, showing Nora a new house and stoking speculation whenever she can. In the meantime she's gettin' it on with Detective Chamberland because he's a silver fox *and* can keep the Brannocks at bay. Of course, karma is just around the corner for Karen, but even then, her exit from her newly acquired house is epic.

Jennifer and showrunner Ryan Murphy weren't strangers: her two-episode turn as Whitney S. Pierce on Murphy's juggernaut series *Glee* back in 2015 was truly unforgettable, and Murphy likes to employ actors in multiple projects. Hopefully Jennifer is on her way to becoming a Murphy mainstay, because Karen Calhoun truly is the best part of *The Watcher*. Jen is in Full Jen Mode, positively conquering every syllable of her dialogue, strutting around in pink blazers and skintight skirts, and, in Karen's final appearance in the series, running down the middle of the street screaming in fluffy mules and a fabulous floral robe. No one else could so perfectly portray flamboyance and fear!

Jen shows us that although you wouldn't want Karen Calhoun to be your friend—Karen Calhoun *has no friends*, only associates—in a series full of jump scares, creepy neighbors, and haunted house realness, she is both much-needed comic relief and the ultimate power-bitch who may as well have "watch your back" tattooed on her posterior.

Jennifer first encountered Ryan Murphy during the filming of *American Horror Story: Coven*—no, you didn't miss her in the series; she let Murphy shoot a scene on the lawn of her New Orleans house. Nearly a decade later Murphy offered Jen the role of Karen Calhoun, one considerably more insidious and conniving than the daffy, goofy ladies Jennifer was known for playing. Naturally, Jennifer hit it out of the park, bringing a dark humor and cutthroat style to Karen, as well as razor-sharp motivations and a wit that threatens to take down a whole suburb. Even if haunted-house thrillers aren't your bag, *The Watcher* is well worth watching for the phenomenon that is Jennifer Coolidge as Karen Calhoun.

Karen is yet another character that shows off Jennifer's mind-blowing versatility and gift for character. While *2 Broke Girls*' Sophie Kachinsky was a ditzy yet loving butterfly of a lady, *The Watcher*'s Karen is a poison dart frog: colorful, vivacious, and positively deadly. Thanks to *The Watcher*, Jen can add a domestic horror series to her bottomless bag of tricks, and hopefully this won't be the last we see of Karen Calhoun. As of this writing, *The Watcher* has been renewed for a second season, and as Karen survived all seven episodes of season one (could we technically call Jen a Final Girl now?), let's hope she returns—spiky shoes, straightened locks, and all.

## FUN BONUS FACTS

✳ In an early trailer for *The Watcher*, Jennifer as Karen hosts an open house video tour of the series' haunted house, with trademark snark *and* flair. Who *wouldn't* buy a house from this foul-mouthed real estate diva?

✳ Horror legend Mia Farrow, who played the Brannocks' oddball neighbor Pearl Winslow on *The Watcher*, wrote about Jennifer when the latter was named one of *TIME* magazine's "100 Most Influential People" of 2023. Farrow wrote, "So many of the qualities that have made everyone fall in love with her [Jen] are outside of what is mainstream or expected: Her eccentric mannerisms, hilarious improvisations, and, most of all, aching vulnerability. She is uncompromisingly, exquisitely herself. Jennifer's honesty and kindness make her a friend anyone would be lucky to have."

# Tanya McQuoid

### *The White Lotus* (2021–2022)

### NOTABLE QUOTABLES

*"These gays! They're trying to murder me!"*

------------

*"Oh my god, am I feeding my mother to the fishes?"*

------------

*"I was told that the cheese here was made by a blind nun in a basement."*

Tanya McQuoid arrives at The White Lotus, a glamorous resort in Maui so exclusive it's only accessible by boat, as a woman on a mission. She's recently lost her mother and wants to spread Mom's ashes during her stay. However, while Tanya has all the money in the world—thanks to being the daughter of a high-profile publishing magnate—she hasn't *quiiiiiiite* processed her grief for the woman with whom she had a very complex relationship, which is likely why Tanya has a full-on breakdown when spa employee Belinda (Natasha Rothwell) can't book her for a massage that very day. Tanya is so distraught that Belinda guides Tanya through a chant and calms her significantly.

Because Belinda is so kind and empathetic, Tanya takes a special interest in the other woman, taking her to dinner—"Are you enjoying your shrimp tacos?" Tanya queries at the table—and offering to fund Belinda's very own spa. Keep in mind that Tanya is a guest and Belinda is an employee, so the class and power differences are . . . uncomfortable, to say the least. However, guests of The White Lotus know no boundaries, and Tanya needs a friend.

While Belinda harbors hope, Tanya engages in what can only be called *shenanigans*. People-pleasing manager Armond (Murray Bartlett) is currently in a battle of wills with entitled honeymooning husband Shane Patton (Jake Lacy) and Shane's meddling mother, Kitty (Molly Shannon), over the availability of the coveted Pineapple Suite. After being insulted yet again, Armond orchestrates a romantic dinner for Shane and his new bride, Rachel (Alexandra Daddario), on the same boat that Tanya has chartered to finally spread her late mother's ashes.

Shane and Rachel are *juuuuust* starting to rekindle the flame when Tanya decides it's time to eulogize. As the young couple, plus the long-suffering Belinda and fellow employee Dillon (Lukas Gage), look on in bemusement, horror, and finally a bit of empathy, Tanya laments the mother she's lost. No, Mama McQuoid wasn't perfect. According to Tanya, her mother had borderline personality disorder, invited way too many men into her bed, possessed no maternal instinct, and wouldn't let Tanya be a ballerina—even when she was skinny. And yet Tanya loves and misses her. Tanya concludes this memorable eulogy by exclaiming, "And what's weird is, I miss my mother, even though she was a big jerk!"

With Shane's help, Tanya opens the elaborate box containing the ashes, but she is only able to scatter a few handfuls of her mother when she decides she is just not ready. By now Dillon, Rachel, and Belinda (and possibly Shane, behind his cool-guy sunglasses) are noticeably moved, and Tanya is inconsolable.

Properly grieved out for the rest of the trip (thanks so much, Armond, and sorry not sorry, newlyweds), Tanya is able to concentrate her energy on more carnal pursuits. She clocks the arrival of affable bachelor of a certain age Greg Hunt (Jon Gries) and is intrigued. When Greg notices Tanya back, the latter cancels plans with Belinda to hang out with her new crush.

But, as Tanya justifies to Belinda, it's totally cool because Greg works for BLM! That means Black Lives Matter, right? Sadly no, Greg is on staff for the Bureau of Land Management, but by the time she learns that, a smitten Tanya pays a nighttime visit to his room.

Sadly, there will be no spa for Belinda, though she *does* survive the week at The White Lotus, which is more than we can say for poor Armond, who finds himself in the Pineapple Suite at the wrong time. While Belinda continues to entertain the whims of wealthy lotus eaters, Tanya flies away with Greg, who by now has revealed that he is terminally ill. This, however, is not the last we will see of the happy—for now—couple.

Season two of *The White Lotus* takes place at the resort's location in Sicily. There's an eclectic new cast of characters—world-weary staffers, beautiful and chaotic locals, and the rich tourists looking to have the experience of their lives—with two notable exceptions. That's right: Tanya McQuoid is *back*. Now Tanya McQuoid-Hunt, she's tied the knot with Greg—though he's signed a hefty prenup—and her endless funds have prolonged the life he thought was almost over when the couple met on Maui.

Tanya, whose White Lotus status has now been upgraded to the ultra-exclusive Blossom Circle, is eager for another unforgettable trip *and* the opportunity to reconnect with her husband. Maybe Greg is hoping for the same, because he's less than thrilled that Tanya brought along her assistant, Portia (Haley Lu Richardson), a scatterbrained twentysomething whose fashion sense resembles Lizzie McGuire's. No worries, Tanya assures Greg, she'll get rid of Portia—which she does, sort of. Portia is instructed to stay in her own room until further notice.

After a less-than-stellar first night, in which Greg accuses Tanya of eating all the free macarons even though she most definitely did *not*, he offers to do whatever she wants all day. Tanya wants to live her Italian movie dreams: riding on a Vespa like in a James Bond film while fetchingly accessorized with a long pink scarf in her hair, and then going out for a big plate of pasta with giant clams. It's everything she hoped for and more—minus the part where Portia and her new friend, Albie (Adam

DiMarco), show up at the same restaurant . . . how dare they!—until Greg breaks the news that he must go back to Denver to deal with a work issue.

Tanya is heartbroken, and Greg is frustrated. He's got to work. Greg impatiently assures Tanya that *yes*, he still loves her. (Even if he didn't, he's not going to leave her, because the ironclad prenup wouldn't be profitable for him.)

Greg departs the next morning, and Portia, who considers Tanya a "miserable mess," is once again a reluctant ear for Tanya's woes. Tanya decides to hire a local fortune teller and summons Portia back from her road trip with Albie and his family to sit with her. While Portia hangs out in the bathroom per Tanya's instruction, the fortune teller seeks to answer the question: Does Greg still love Tanya? Though the tarot cards initially predict deceit and beauty, the fortune teller begins babbling in Italian. Tanya is *thoroughly* unsatisfied, calls the fortune teller a "con artist," and kicks her out of the room. At dinner Tanya warns Portia against emotionally unavailable men before sadly making her way back to her room—but not before a table full of well-dressed men wave and smile.

The next morning Tanya wonders if her loneliness is karmic payback for *not* helping a certain White Lotus employee start a spa for poor people back on Maui. Tanya speculates: Could "that girl" have put a curse on her? Before Portia can make heads or tails of this non sequitur (and season one callback), both boss and assistant are swept away by a group Tanya will heretofore refer to as "the gays."

These gays are not actually guests at The White Lotus. In fact, the quartet of snappily attired European flatterers don't reveal much about

themselves at all, but that doesn't matter to Tanya, because they're giving her what she wants most: *attention*. Magnetic British expat Quentin (Tom Hollander) probes Tanya for details of her life while plying her with rosé and appetizers as his handsome nephew, Jack (Leo Woodall), works his considerable charms on Portia. Everyone is getting along so fabulously that Quentin invites both Tanya and Portia to stay for two nights at his villa in nearby Palermo. Surely there's no ulterior motive in getting these two away from the safety of the resort, right?

"Don't steal anything!" Tanya furiously whispers to Portia as the two of them enter Quentin's villa—both jaw-droppingly stunning and noticeably crumbling—after a ride on a lush yacht (as Tanya observes, "These are some high-end gays!"). Quentin and the gays sweep Tanya away for a night at the opera: the tragedy *Madama Butterfly*, a story of dying for love. Tanya even thinks she spies the Queen of Sicily in one of the box seats—so exciting! It's truly a beautiful night, which ends with a nightcap and bonding between Tanya and Quentin.

The latter confesses he hasn't fallen in love since his younger days, when a cowboy from the States stole his heart. Now he's only committed to beauty, even if that means dying for it. They drink a toast to beauty, and Tanya heads to bed, only to encounter a rude awakening in the middle of the night: after hearing noises, she accidentally stumbles upon Quentin locked in an embrace with none other than his "nephew," Jack. They do not notice her watching them.

The next morning Tanya does her best to warn a besotted Portia that Jack may not be who he seems, but she can't bring herself to share the intimate details of what she witnessed. She and Portia are soon distracted:

Jack whisks Portia away for an "adventure," and Quentin proposes a party that evening in Tanya's honor. While Tanya is feted—Quentin even provides a strapping younger man for her, who feeds her cocaine *and* takes her to bed—Portia grows disillusioned with an increasingly drunk Jack.

At the end of the night Jack gets a hotel room for the two of them and makes a completely inebriated confession: Quentin is broke and on the verge of losing his villa but is about to come into "a windfall," and Jack owes Quentin for getting him out of a very dark place. Before she is bedded by the younger, handsome man, Tanya finds a photo on Quentin's dresser . . . of a younger Quentin alongside a man who is most definitely Tanya's absent husband, Greg Hunt.

The next morning Tanya and Portia are separated, unsettled, and very eager to get back to The White Lotus. After vaguely putting off Tanya when she asks him about the photo of Greg, Quentin boards the yacht with Tanya and the gays, ostensibly heading back to the resort, though the ship's captain drops anchor in the middle of the water, leaving them stranded. Thanks to a frantic call from Portia, Tanya is apprised of Jack's late-night confession, and the two put together that Greg likely knows Quentin and orchestrated this entire scheme to get rid of Tanya. After all, if they divorce, Greg gets no money, but if Tanya dies . . .

Tanya is convinced that, as she proclaims to the beleaguered non-English-speaking ship's captain, "These gays, they're trying to murder me!" Knowing she is trapped, Tanya tries to keep her cool, even when last night's lover, Niccoló (Stefano Gianino)—who has ties to the mob—arrives, bearing a mysterious black bag and promising to escort her back to The White Lotus after they all have dinner together.

Eventually Tanya makes a run for it, grabbing Niccoló's black bag and locking herself in a bedroom on the yacht. She discovers the bag contains duct tape, rope, and a gun—these gays are, indeed, trying to murder her. When Quentin breaks down the door, a furious *and* frightened Tanya blindly shoots, obliterating him and almost all the murderous gays (one escapes and jumps overboard)—but how can Tanya get to the lifeboat below the yacht?

"You got this," Tanya assures herself, but before she can figure out how to jump, her heeled shoe catches on the railing and Tanya tumbles to her death in the depths of the sea in the dark night.

The next morning, unsuspecting White Lotus guest Daphne (Meghann Fahy) takes one last dip in the ocean and bumps into the body of one Tanya McQuoid-Hunt, who never found the true love she so desperately craved. Portia also didn't make it back to The White Lotus, but in a moment of conscience, Jack let her off at the airport the night before. While waiting for her flight, Portia meets Albie again and learns that a White Lotus guest has drowned. Portia, of course, knows this is the end of Tanya McQuoid-Hunt.

## Why We Heart Tanya

How do we love Tanya McQuoid, and Jennifer as Tanya McQuoid? Let us count the ways!

Simply put, Tanya McQuoid is so wrong she's right. She never quite says or does the correct thing, whether she's mistaking Bureau of Land Management for Black Lives Matter, or publicly breaking down in front of a newly married couple in the middle of the ocean, or trusting the wrong group of fabulous gay men. Not to mention, a seasoned traveler probably *wouldn't* request Oreo cookie cake at a Sicilian breakfast buffet.

But these never-ending gaffes are precisely what make Tanya McQuoid so eminently watchable. The classic "no filter" lady, Tanya can't *not* say what's on her mind or express every emotion she has the second she has it. Towering over all White Lotus guests, staff, and management in every sense of the word, Tanya is a fascinating character because you're never quite sure what she's going to do next. She's also a walking, talking, sobbing lesson in karma: we know Belinda didn't put a curse on her, but we do wonder if Tanya's Sicilian demise is, in fact, retribution for abandoning the White Lotus employee who was genuinely kind to her.

Jennifer as Tanya? Legendary. Mike White was inspired to write the character after going on vacation with Jennifer and witnessing her genuine quirkiness in full force. Though, of course, Jennifer isn't *actually* Tanya, she is the only person who could bring Tanya's observations, mannerisms, and caftan-rific style to life. More than that, Jennifer brings depth to a character who may have transformed into a one-note caricature in the hands of a less talented actress. Everything Tanya does comes across as completely genuine because Jennifer has made it so. She doesn't judge Tanya; she *becomes* her.

Thanks to Jennifer's bravura performance, we may not always feel like Tanya, but we feel *for* her. Who among us hasn't mourned a loved one who played a complicated role in our own lives, or made promises we couldn't keep, or put our faith in a person who didn't have our best interests at heart? Tanya McQuoid may not be the most likable of Jennifer Coolidge's characters, but she is the most deeply human, and Jennifer brings every ounce of her experience, creativity, and straight-up talent to her interpretation. Thanks to Jennifer, Tanya McQuoid is one of a kind—always hilarious, often frustrating, and someone who we can empathize with, root for, and yell, "For the love of god, wear different shoes!"

## FUN BONUS FACTS

✦ Remember how we all felt during COVID—scared, hopeless, depressed? Jennifer felt that way too, and she used it for Tanya when filming *The White Lotus*'s first season. "I just was watching way too much of the news and reading way too many sad stories," she said in an interview with *The Ringer*. "I felt it very strongly as the most vulnerable I've ever felt in my life."

✦ Tanya's impromptu eulogy of her late mother, delivered to the unwilling audience of Shane and Rachel, was not only partly improvised—essentially writer and creator Mike White told her to go for it—but it was also delivered under less-than-ideal circumstances. "I just got so immensely seasick, and we had to shoot on a boat," Jennifer told *The Ringer* in 2021, referring to this scene. "I got just deathly ill on the boat. The boat was too small, so they didn't really have conditions where you could go and use the restroom, so they just gave me a bucket. The rest . . . of the cast members were on the boat, and I was right next to them delivering lines and then heaving into my bucket!" However, Jennifer added, "It was all worth it."

✳ Jennifer has cast a wide net in New York, Los Angeles, and beyond: once you know to look for connections, you will find them everywhere. In seasons one and two of *The White Lotus*, Tanya's love interest-turned-spouse, Greg Hunt, is played by Jon Gries, who had a prominent role as dastardly ex–high school football player Uncle Rico in *Napoleon Dynamite*—cowritten and directed by Jared Hess, who also directed Jennifer in *Gentlemen Broncos*.

✳ The role of Tanya McQuoid on *The White Lotus* was an absolute game changer for Jennifer. In 2022 she earned her first Emmy®, and in 2023 she received a Golden Globe Award® and two SAG (Screen Actors Guild) Awards® and was honored at the 2023 MTV Movie & TV Awards with the Comic Genius Award. She also received a special honor at the 2023 GLAAD Awards®. At sixty-two, she is having a career renaissance—or, as *Vogue* calls it, a *Jenaissance*!

# FUN FACTS ABOUT JEN!

Naturally, such a fascinating character onscreen is equally so off camera. Here are a few fun facts about Ms. Coolidge, from her most famous ancestor to her animal advocacy to the place she calls home.

Jennifer didn't only study acting. Before making it big, she took courses in special effects, fashion, and beauty at LA's Joe Blasco School. Part of the curriculum included a mortuary makeup class. "I was very nervous about the mortuary makeup part, but it turned out we didn't work on any bodies or anything—it was all sort of virtual," Jennifer told *Vogue*. "We never had to actually do it on a corpse. It wouldn't be my first choice."

—————————

Jennifer loves to dress up. She told *Us Weekly*, "I probably have more costumes than regular clothes." Is it any surprise that her favorite holiday is Halloween?

—————————

Jennifer does her best to eat vegan, but as she shared with E. Alex Jung of *Vulture*, "It's difficult on film sets or when there are so many delicious things, like aged Camembert butter and crab claws."

—————————

According to an interview with *Us Weekly*, Jennifer is related to President Calvin Coolidge—she's his sixth cousin, twice removed. (Could a stint in the White House be next for our queen? It runs in the family, after all!)

—————————

Jennifer has told several press outlets about her love for bubble gum. She says, "Sometimes I try to figure out how many pieces of gum I can fit into my mouth at once." She also told *Deadline*, "I like to buy a big bag of bubble gum and chew it for two seconds and put it on my nightstand. I can go through the whole bag. I don't know, it's like it's something really decadent."

———————

One of Jennifer's earliest roles was in *Bucket of Blood*, a TV remake of a film directed by the B-movie king behind the original *Little Shop of Horrors*, none other than Roger Corman. The work, however, was less than glamorous. "I'm not even given a name in that one. I'm called 'stupid girl' in the credits," Jennifer told the *Atlanta Journal-Constitution's Radio & TV Talk* blog in 2009. "I think I got paid $700 take-home for that one!"

———————

If you ever meet Jennifer and would like to give her a bouquet, take note: her favorite flowers are peonies.

———————

The oddest of odd jobs Jennifer's ever had? An undercover shopper . . . with a very special condition. "When I was in Florida, I got a job as an undercover pregnant woman looking for shoplifters at a maternity store," Jennifer told *Deadline* in 2022. And because this is Jennifer Coolidge we're talking about, there's a plot twist. She went on to reveal: "The irony of the story is that I caught the cashier stealing, not one of the shoppers."

———————

Morning glory? Not even! Jennifer tells *Us Weekly*, "I was born without energy, so everyday [sic] involves at least 12 shots of espresso."

———————

Jennifer's true passion is animals. According to *Us Weekly*, her dog Chuy was rescued from a meat factory in Korea, via the Animal Rescue Mission. *Vulture* shares that Jennifer has another dog named Bagpipes, who she enjoys photoshopping into her pictures. And best of all, PETA (People for the Ethical Treatment of Animals) has officially crowned Jennifer its 2023 Vegan Queen, an honor Jennifer enthusiastically shared on her Instagram.

# MATCH GAME:
# MORE NOTABLE QUOTABLES

Time for an open-book test! Throughout this book we've listed popular quotes for each of Jennifer's most memorable characters. Match the character with the quote below (for extra credit—and to make Jen proud—don't check the book).

___ 1)  *"How can you tell if a guy is gay?"*

___ 2)  *"Eat a d\*ck, Stephanie!"*

___ 3)  *"My snap was all over the place!"*

___ 4)  *"Those act as flippers."*

___ 5)  *"Mister Finch, are you trying to seduce me?"*

___ 6)  *"Thank God for the model trains. If they didn't have the model trains, they wouldn't have gotten the idea for the big trains."*

Ⓐ **SHERRI ANN CABOT,**
*Best in Show*

Ⓑ **PAULETTE BONAFONTÉ,**
*Legally Blonde*

Ⓒ **BOBBIE ST. BROWN,**
*Party Down*

Ⓓ **AMBER COLE,**
*A Mighty Wind*

Ⓔ **STIFLER'S MOM,**
*American Pie*

Ⓕ **KAREN CALHOUN,**
*The Watcher*

___ 7) *"People who use extra water have extra class!"*

___ 8) *"I'll be in my booth!"*

___ 9) *"I'm gonna look great in those wench gowns."*

___ 10) *"No more rest home readings. The food always sucks!"*

___ 11) *"Hi, guys! Did you catch any neat rocks?"*

___ 12) *"And that's why blondes don't necessarily have more fun!"*

___ 13) *"Oh my god, am I feeding my mother to the fishes?"*

**G** MISS ELIZABETH CHARMING,
*Austenland*

**H** TANYA MCQUOID,
*The White Lotus*

**I** JUDY ROMANO,
*We Have a Ghost*

**J** SOPHIE KACHINSKY,
*2 Broke Girls*

**K** MISS KREMZER,
*King of the Hill*

**L** FIONA MONTGOMERY,
*A Cinderella Story*

**M** JUDITH PURVIS,
*Gentlemen Broncos*

# WHICH JENNIFER COOLIDGE CHARACTER ARE YOU?

Jennifer has played a host of legendary characters. Even her TV guest appearances were infused with comedy gold—and as movies like *Promising Young Woman* show, she's got a gift for drama as well. Have you ever wondered, *If I were a Jennifer Coolidge character, who would I be?* Worry no more, and take this quiz to find out once and for all.

**1)** **Time to get ready for the day ahead! What will you be wearing to present your best self?**

Ⓐ Likely more than one outfit: a tight miniskirt for swanning around your mansion, a puffy coat for horsing around with your, um, *friend* and her dogs, and a majestic evening gown. You may not have a job, but you are *busy*. Also, marabou is an important part of *every* outfit.

Ⓑ A fitted power suit and high heels because you've got hustling to do. Unless of course, you are playing tennis with your old pal and yelling insults at Stephanie. She knows what she did.

Ⓒ Denim everything, topped off with a scrunchie. Possibly some flower print. Cute yet functional and eye-catching to a certain man with a package . . .

**D** One of your many caftans, one of your many large hats, and one of your many pairs of giant sunglasses. All black, or possibly salmon, because a gay man told you how amazing you look in it, and he has no ulterior motive at all!

## 2) What's your very favorite food?

**A** Soup, if you're having dinner with your husband. Shrimp cocktail, if you're feeling fancy. But when you're stressed, you'll take a large bucket of popcorn, half butter, half salt.

**B** A salad that you will pick at while trying to get the dirt on who's buying what and who's doing whom, which you will wash down with a "holiday pour" of white wine. And absolutely no baked goods—you're doing keto now.

**C** A donut. You can eat it with one hand while reading a magazine with the other in your downtime. Plus, sweet pastry is perfect if you're happy *or* sad!

**D** Whatever they're serving on the specially chartered boat while you're carefully guarding your mother's ashes. Or cheese made by a blind nun in a basement!

## 3) You're on the hunt for a special man. Pick your "type":

**A** Old, rich, loves snow peas, and talking and not talking. Physical to the point of *you* having to push *him* away!

**B** The world of the suburbs is your oyster, and your type knows no limits. Could be your college friend's gorgeous husband, who's clearly not getting enough at home. Could be your sexy boss. Could be the silver fox of the local police detective. The more verboten the better . . . except for Rick Bluck, because been there, done that, and *eww*.

**C** You need a man who can handle a big package while rocking snug brown shorts and who doesn't mind if you accidentally break his nose.

**D** Works for BLM—*which* BLM doesn't really matter. Leaves you to your own devices, which may include running around with flamboyant gay men who absolutely have *no* ulterior motive for you or your bottom-less wealth.

## 4) Choose your dream career:

**A** Bankrolling a dog kennel, thus elevating it from shitbox to state-of-the-art facility. And if you get to spend extra time with your purebred poodle's female trainer, all the better.

**B** Real estate agent who specializes in big old houses that may or may not be haunted. You are all about that fat commission.

**C** Manicurist. Who knows what blonde law student friends you'll make today? Plus, your beloved dog can come to work with you—after you get him back from your icky ex, that is. You might even learn to bend and snap!

**D** You *would* have been a ballerina if your now-dead mother hadn't forbidden it. Dammit.

**5)** If you could go anywhere on vacation, where would that be?

Ⓐ Either the dog show where your pooch will *absolutely* win for the third year in a row, or a scouting trip for your new magazine, *American Bitch*. As long as your lady friend is by your side, you will have a grand time!

Ⓑ A beige room that your interior decorator just finished, because you are a single girl who takes care of herself.

Ⓒ Wherever you go, it better be on the Fourth of July, and there better be hot dogs.

Ⓓ An exclusive resort that will cater to your every whim, with worldwide locations and endless shenanigans. And you might just venture outside of it because your new gay friends—who, again, have no ulterior motive whatsoever—invited you on their glorious boat!

## If your answers were mostly A's you are . . . Sherri Ann Cabot!

You have it all: buckets of wealth, a lovely place to lay your head, and endless adoration from your spouse, your "best friend," and your prize-winning pet. Most of all, you have the gift of time, and you can use it however you want—whether that's appearing on a local talk show, doing your best friend's hair and makeup, or chowing down on popcorn. In short, you are fabulous.

### If your answers were mostly B's you are . . .
### Karen Calhoun!

Your hometown may be small, but your power and influence are *massive*. You can unload a house, have an affair, and do cardio all in the same afternoon. While everyone else is worrying about scary stalkers or marital fidelity, you are out there *doing*—whether that's raking in money or getting your carnal needs met. Your power suits are fitted, your heels high, and your confidence in the stratosphere. In short, you are fabulous.

### If your answers were mostly C's you are . . .
### Paulette Bonafonté!

Maybe your beginnings weren't so great, and you've had some significant challenges to overcome. Sooner or later you surrounded yourself with people who lift you up—and maybe did a bend and snap or two. In doing so, you unlocked the key to your own beautiful sense of self and found the love you deserved. You did it! Also, you treasure furry friends. In short, you are fabulous.

### If your answers were mostly D's you are . . .
### Tanya McQuoid!

You follow your heart, even when those around you don't *quite* understand what you're doing or why. Well, it's not their life, is it? You fall in like and in love easily, which is incredibly charming, even when it's also frustrating to others. You are both complex and endlessly whimsical, which is why everyone's fascinated by you. Just be careful of ulterior motives! In short, you are fabulous.

# ACKNOWLEDGMENTS

First and foremost, thank you thank you thank you to my editor extraordinaire, Jordana Hawkins. From *Queer Eye* to *Screaming Goat* to *Clueless* to the divine J. Cool, I always have an absolute blast working with you. Here's to many more!

Thank you to Leah Gordon, Josephine Moore, Shannon Fabricant, and everyone at Running Press and Hachette Book Group for making this whole process so smooth and—dare I say—fun.

Thank you to Evan Ross Katz, whose *White Lotus* memes always crack me up *and* educate me, and whose interview with Jennifer was both eye-opening and fabulous.

Thank you to Blake Kimzey of Writing Workshops, who sat with me at a breakfast table in Iceland and listened to my twenty-minute rave about the glorious character of Karen Calhoun. Iceland was pretty cool too.

Thank you to my coauthor and friend, Lillah Lawson, who picked up the slack on our novel's final edits while I was binge-watching season two of *The White Lotus*. You're my favorite person to exchange voicemails with.

Thank you to Rob Cameron, who's had my back since the very first first draft of a short story I wrote when we were twentysomething roommates in Chicago.

Thank you to my family, especially Mom and Meghan, with whom I watched *Legally Blonde* that first time in the theater—and many times since.

And of course, thank you, Jennifer Coolidge. Your presence among us mere mortals is nothing short of joyful.

# SOURCES

Allaire, Christian. "Welcome to the Jenaissance." *Vogue*, October 26, 2022. Accessed March 1, 2023.

Blyth, Antonia. "On My Screen: 'White Lotus' Star Jennifer Coolidge on Her Most-Quoted Role, the Part She Didn't Get to Play & Why 'Character Is Fate.'" *Deadline*, August 13, 2022. Accessed March 1, 2023.

Brown, Evan Nicole. "Jennifer Coolidge and 'White Lotus' Creator Mike White Reteam for e.l.f. Cosmetics Super Bowl Ad." *The Hollywood Reporter*, February 12, 2023. Accessed March 7, 2023.

Calfee, Joel. "Jennifer Coolidge Left This Surprise Video on J.Lo's Phone During the Filming of 'Shotgun Wedding.'" *PureWow*, January 29, 2023. Accessed June 14, 2023.

Coolidge, Jennifer. *Internet Movie Database* profile. Accessed March 1, 2023.

Dweck, Sophie, and Kat Pettibone. "Jennifer Coolidge: 25 Things You Don't Know About Me ('I Probably Have More Costumes Than Regular Clothes!')." *Us Weekly*, February 27, 2023. Accessed March 1, 2023.

Farrow, Mia. "The 100 Most Influential People of 2023: Jennifer Coolidge." *Time*, April 13, 2023. Accessed April 14, 2023.

Frank, Jason P. "A Comprehensive List of Everything Jennifer Coolidge Does in *The Watcher*." *Vulture*, October 18, 2022. Accessed March 1, 2023.

Hawgood, Alex. "Jennifer Coolidge Will Destroy You." *W Magazine*, March 1, 2023. Accessed March 7, 2023.

Herman, Alison. "Jennifer Coolidge Wants You to Know Mike White Is a Genius." *The Ringer*, August 2, 2021. Accessed March 1, 2023.

Ho, Rodney. "Interview with Jennifer Coolidge (Stifler's Mom), at Laughing Skull Lounge July 23–26." *Atlanta Journal-Constitution*, July 22, 2009. Accessed March 1, 2023.

Hullender, Tatiana. "Jennifer Coolidge Interview: *Promising Young Woman*." *Screen Rant*, April 9, 2021. Accessed March 7, 2023.

Jung, E. Alex. "The Joke Was Never on Jennifer Coolidge." *New York Magazine/Vulture*, July 5, 2021. Accessed March 7, 2023.

Kaplan, Ilana. "'Legally Blonde' Oral History: From Raunchy Script to Feminist Classic." *New York Times,* July 8, 2021. Accessed May 30, 2023.

Katz, Evan Ross, host. "Jennifer Coolidge." *Shut Up Evan,* Acast, February 1, 2022. Accessed March 7, 2023.

Korducki, Kelli María. "The Midlife Renaissance of Women in Hollywood." *The Atlantic,* February 7, 2023. Accessed March 7, 2023.

Maron, Marc, host. "Episode 790: Jennifer Coolidge." *WTF with Marc Maron,* Acast, March 1, 2017. Accessed March 1, 2023.

Nemetz, Dave. "Anatomy of an Emmy-Worthy Scene: *The White Lotus'* Jennifer Coolidge Reveals How Seasick She Got Shooting Tanya's Emotional Boat Eulogy." *TVLine,* June 24, 2022. Accessed May 18, 2023.

Olsen, Mark, and Yvonne Villareal, hosts. "Jennifer Coolidge Welcomes Her Closeup." *The Envelope, Los Angeles Times,* August 5, 2022. Accessed March 7, 2023.

Paul, Larisha. "Jennifer Coolidge's Dreams Were Once 'Fizzled Out by Life.' Now She's the Star of the Golden Globes." *Rolling Stone,* January 11, 2023. Accessed April 25, 2023.

Rubenstein, Jeanine. "Jennifer Coolidge Jokes She's 'Surrounded by Gays' Before Receiving GLAAD Award from Jane Lynch." *People,* March 31, 2023. Accessed April 25, 2023.

Singh, Olivia. "*The White Lotus* Showrunner Mike White Unpacks the 'Derpy Death' on the Season 2 Finale." *Insider,* December 12, 2022. Accessed May 13, 2023.

Squires, Bethy. "*American Pie* Got Jennifer Coolidge Hella Laid." *Vulture,* August 3, 2022. Accessed March 7, 2023.

Van Paris, Calin. "Jennifer Coolidge on TikTok Beauty Tutorials, 'Baby Dolphin' Skin, and Her #GRWM-Inspired Super Bowl Commercial." *Vogue,* February 9, 2023. Accessed May 22, 2023.

Zellner, Sarah. "The Ultimate Guide to Jennifer Coolidge as Sophie in *2 Broke Girls.*" *The Things,* January 11, 2023. Accessed April 22, 2023.

# ABOUT THE AUTHOR

**LAUREN EMILY WHALEN** writes fiction for teens and adults, including the novels *Take Her Down, Two Winters,* and *Tomorrow and Tomorrow* (cowritten with Lillah Lawson). Her articles have appeared in *SELF, Bust,* and *GO* magazines, and she is a regular reviewer for and contributor to *Kirkus Reviews, BookPage,* and Q.Digital. She is also the author of *Queer Eye: Find the Fab Five: A Totally Fierce Seek-and-Find, Queer Eye: You Are Fabulous: A Fill-In Book, Queer Eye: Talking Button, Clueless Magnet Set,* and *The Screaming Christmas Goat.* Lauren lives in Chicago with her cat, Rosaline, and an apartment full of books, and she never misses a Jennifer Coolidge show! Say hello at laurenemilywrites.com.

# ABOUT THE ILLUSTRATOR

**NERYL WALKER** is an Australian artist, illustrator, and designer who loves to celebrate women. Inspired by a love of mid-twentieth-century pop culture, her studio and 1950s home are filled with countless sources of vintage and nostalgic inspiration. While she is best known for her illustrations of strong, playful girls, Neryl's background in graphic design has also seen her collaborating on branding, typography, surface design, and publishing projects.